119661

D1555434

BEACON
BIBLE
EXPOSITIONS

BEACON BIBLE EXPOSITIONS

BEACON BIBLE EXPOSITIONS

VOLUME 8

GALATIANS
EPHESIANS

by
WILLARD H. TAYLOR

Editors
WILLIAM M. GREATHOUSE
WILLARD H. TAYLOR

BEACON HILL PRESS OF KANSAS CITY
Kansas City, Missouri

Copyright, 1981
Beacon Hill Press of Kansas City

ISBN: 0-8341-0734-1

Library of Congress Catalog Card No. 74-78052

Printed in the
United States of America

Contents

Editors' Preface

No Christian preacher or teacher has been more aware of the creating and sustaining power of the Word of God than the apostle Paul. As a strategem in his missionary endeavors, he sought out synagogues in the major cities where he knew Jews would gather to hear the Old Testament. No doubt he calculated that he would be invited to expound the Scriptures and so he would have a golden opportunity to preach Christ. That peripatetic preacher was confident that valid Christian experience and living could not be enjoyed apart from the Word of God, whether preached or written. To the Thessalonians he wrote: "And we also thank God constantly for this, that when you received the word of God which you heard from us, you accepted it not as the word of men but as what it really is, the word of God, which is at work in you believers" (1 Thess. 2:13, RSV). Strong Christians—and more broadly, strong churches—are born of, and nurtured on, authentic and winsome exposition of the Bible.

Beacon Bible Expositions provide a systematic, devotional Bible study program for laymen and a fresh, homiletical resource for preachers. All the benefits of the best biblical scholarship are found in them, but nontechnical language is used in the composition. A determined effort is made to relate the clarified truth to life today. The writers, Wesleyan in theological perspective, seek to interpret the gospel, pointing to the Living Word, Christ, who is the primary Subject of all scripture, the Mediator of redemption, and the Norm of Christian living.

The publication of this series is a prayerful invitation to both laymen and ministers to set out on a lifelong, systematic study of the Bible. Hopefully these studies will supply the initial impetus.

—WILLIAM M. GREATHOUSE AND
WILLARD H. TAYLOR, *Editors*

The Epistle to the
GALATIANS

Topical Outline of Galatians

Salutation (1:1-5)

> Paul, a True Apostle (1:1-2)
> The Blessing (1:3-5)

The Authenticity of Paul's Gospel (1:6—2:21)

> No Other Gospel (1:6-10)
> By Special Revelation (1:11-12)
> Attested in His Remarkable Experience (1:13-24)
> Vindicated Finally by the Jerusalem Leaders (2:1-10)
> Consistency in Witness (2:11-13)
> Grace Means Freedom (2:14-21)

The Proof of History (3:1—4:31)

> The Spirit as a Gift of Faith (3:1-5)
> Abraham, the Father of Faith (3:6-9)
> Deliverance from the Curse of the Law (3:10-14)
> The Unalterable Covenant (3:15-18)
> The Real Purpose of the Law (3:19-22)
> The New Order of Faith (3:23-29)
> What Heirship Means (4:1-7)
> Falling into Slavery (4:8-11)
> An Appeal from the Heart (4:12-20)
> An Old Testament Lesson (4:21-31)

The Life of Freedom (5:1-26)

> The Tragedy of Turning Back (5:1-5)
> Love, the Essence of the Free Life (5:6-12)
> Liberty and Love (5:13-15)
> Walking in the Spirit (5:16-18)
> The Harvest of the Spirit (5:19-24)
> Life in the Spirit (5:25-26)

Freedom to Serve Others (6:1-10)

> A Faltering Member (6:1-5)
> Support of Christian Teachers (6:6)
> Sowing and Reaping (6:7-10)

Postscript (6:11-18)

> The Final Salvo (6:11-16)
> The Mark of Authenticity (6:17-18)

Introduction

The genuineness of the Epistle to the Galatians was never questioned in the Early Church, and even the most radical critics of the New Testament have regarded it as unquestionably Pauline. The letter was written, as it states in 1:1, by the apostle Paul. It stands alongside the Epistle to the Romans as one of the "Pillar Epistles" of the Apostle. Thus, the authorship of this letter need not be discussed.

The Recipients

One might conclude upon reading the phrase in 1:2 *unto the churches of Galatia* that the question of who the readers were would be easily settled. However, the location of these churches presents serious problems. Galatia stretched across the central portion of Asia Minor, which is known today as Turkey. The word "Galatia" appears in Acts 16:6 and 18:23 and is used to refer to the southern part of the territory known by that name. According to Acts 14, Paul preached in this area in the cities of Antioch and Iconium, and it would be most natural to assume that his letter was addressed to the congregations in this region. From the earliest centuries of the Church, however, some scholars have insisted that to speak of "Galatia" was to refer to the northern portion of this region where the inhabitants would be more strictly called Galatians, for it was the imperial Roman province by that name, so established in 25 B.C. Two theories as to the recipients have been propounded by scholars: the South Galatian Theory and the North Galatian Theory.

The arguments in defense of both theories are numerous, but it would seem to this writer that the South Galatian Theory is the more plausible one. The Book of Acts, which is our principal source of information on the missionary labors of Paul, contains no explicit reference to his evangelization of the northern region. The indication that the Galatians knew Barnabas, who accompanied Paul on the first missionary journey, carries some weight in the decision (see 2:9, 13). One should not be too dogmatic on this issue, for the arguments for and against each theory merit serious consideration. However, to this author the evidence seems to be on the side of the South Galatian Theory. This would mean that the Epistle, in all likelihood, was written to the churches which Paul, along with Barnabas, established on his first mssion (see 4:13).

The Date

Once again we are confronted with a complex problem. But to have accepted the South Galatian Theory for the destination of the letter, it seems reasonable to settle on a date sometime after the first missionary journey (Acts 14) and before the First Church Council held in Jerusalem (Acts 15). This position assumes that the account of Paul's visit to Jerusalem in Galatians 2 is the same as "the famine visit" recorded in Acts 11:30. The doctrinal controversy which led eventually to the famous Jerusalem Council was beginning to reach a heated stage. If, as others have suggested, the Council had already been held, why did Paul not use the decisions of the Council in his debate with the Galatians? We conclude that the letter was written not too many months before the famous gathering in Jerusalem, generally dated in A.D. 49. And the place of writing was probably Antioch in Syria.

The Purpose

Apparently, after Paul had left the Galatian churches, other so-called Christian missionaries visited them and taught them a different view of the gospel. These "Judaizers," as they have become traditionally known, insisted that to be a good Christian, one had first to become a good Jew. They said that "salvation by faith alone" was only half the truth. Faith in Christ must be accompanied by obedience to the law. Christians, to be true Christians, must submit to the fleshly sign of circumcision (5:2-6; 6:12-15) and bring their lives entirely under the law. When this approach was taken by the Judaizers, they, at the same time, attacked the legitimacy of Paul's apostleship (1:1, 10-24).

The Teachings

In response to the troublers of the Galatians, the Judaizers, Paul, first of all, makes clear that his apostleship and message were independently given him by revelation from God. His message was not "secondhand," passed on to him by others, but nevertheless approved by the church leaders.

Most fundamental, the gospel is one of grace alone through faith in the Christ of Calvary, and is complete in itself. Believers, Jews and Gentiles alike, enjoy in Christ *a complete salvation,* since they are justified (3:6-9), adopted into the family of God (4:4-7), made new creatures (6:15), made heirs according to the promise of the Abrahamic covenant (3:15-18), and live out of the resources of the Spirit (5:16-25). All this means freedom from the frustrating search for salvation by the doing of the works of the law. To return to the law, therefore, would result in the forfeiting of one's freedom in the Spirit (3:1-5; 5:1-12; 6:11-16). Believers must not revert to the principle of law-keeping as the basis of salvation. "Keep the freedom of the Spirit at any cost" is the "bottom line" of the Apostle's message. Christ and His atoning work, received by faith, are sufficient; we need nothing more! Grace, therefore, means freedom in the Spirit.

For our preaching today, Galatians offers a wealth of

ideas: (1) that there is the need to protect Christ's Church from heresy; (2) that the heart of the gospel is one's acceptance of Christ as Lord and Savior and his incorporation into the body of believers; (3) that freedom in the Spirit leads to love and joyful spiritual discipline, not to moral license, and (4) that a life based upon an authentic relationship to God, exerts a powerful influence.

Salutation

Galatians 1:1-5

GALATIANS 1

Paul, a True Apostle

Galatians 1:1-2

> 1 Paul, an apostle, (not of men, neither by man, but by Jesus Christ, and God the Father, who raised him from the dead;)
> 2 And all the brethren which are with me, unto the churches of Galatia:

Apparently the missionaries who traveled through Galatia preaching a perverted gospel also were saying that Paul was not a true apostle. Paul usually introduces himself as an apostle (Rom. 1:1; 1 Cor. 1:1; Eph. 1:1; Col. 1:1), but here he adds a significant parenthesis which emphasizes the validity of his apostleship. He asserts that his apostleship is not derived from human succession nor by the special act of men. That is to say, he was not "elected" to this ministry by ecclesiastical action. Even the "laying on of hands" by Ananias (see Acts 9:17) should not be taken as the origin of his apostleship. Paul firmly believed his apostolic role came *by Jesus Christ* and *God the Father* who raised Jesus from the dead.

Simultaneously with the call of the Risen Christ to salvation came the call to minister to the Gentiles.

We sense the struggle of Paul over this issue as he seeks to establish the truth of the gospel against the false teaching of the Judaizers (see 1:10—2:10). There are two distinguishing marks of his apostleship which say something to us about authentic ministry.

1. *The radical change in his life which accompanied his entry into the apostolate.* The 12 disciples, who composed the first group of apostles, experienced conversion and newness through the immediate ministry of Christ to them, but considering the pre-Christian life of Paul, none of them seem to have experienced the same sharp antithesis between their past and their subsequent ministry for Christ that Paul did and which he was always to declare (see Phil. 3:7 ff). Paul had been whole-souled in his commitment to the law and his persecution of the early Christian community was a defence of the faith. But with his encounter with Jesus on the road to Damascus he turned 180 degrees. There had not been a period of vacillation, as was the case with the other apostles. On the contrary, there was a sudden and resolute commitment to the Messiah Jesus whom he had passionately persecuted. An authentic ministry results when the servant can witness with assurance that the Risen Lord has indeed changed his life and called him into the ministry of the Word.

2. *The recovery of the prophetic spirit which evidenced itself in his ministry throughout his life.* The parallels between Paul and Jeremiah have long been noted. The essential parallel is their utter devotion to the divine will, expressed in an undaunted readiness to suffer for its fulfillment in and through their lives. Paul, like Jeremiah, viewed suffering as a divinely willed element in the life of a true apostle (see 2 Cor. 11:16 ff; 12:10; Gal. 6:17; Phil. 3:10 ff). Moreover, Paul, like Jeremiah, concentrated almost exclusively on the preaching of the Word of the Lord, whatever the consequences (1 Cor. 1:14 ff), and he re-

nounced any ecstatic basis for the apostolate (2 Cor. 12:1 ff).

Being a God-sent messenger is what ministry is all about. Getting the message through, at whatever personal cost, without compromise, and with unshakable confidence in God's Word is the task resting upon the ministry. Today's world desperately needs more "Pauline" apostles!

The Blessing

Galatians 1:3-5

> 3 Grace be to you and peace from God the Father, and from our Lord Jesus Christ,
> 4 Who gave himself for our sins, that he might deliver us from this present evil world, according to the will of God and our Father:
> 5 To whom be glory for ever and ever. Amen.

Along with the persons traveling with him, Paul expresses the wish that his readers experience in special measure the grace and peace of God our Father and the Lord Jesus Christ. Paul rightfully can be called "the apostle of grace and peace."

1. *Grace* is God's gift to sinners of forgiveness and newness of spiritual life. This "favoring" of men who do not deserve it has its origin in the love and mercy of God. This word *grace,* a key to Paul's gospel, expresses the very essence of the Christian life. Christians are people who are living in and by God's grace. "It is by grace you have been saved, through faith—and this not from yourselves, it is the gift of God—not by works, so that no one can boast" (Eph. 2:8-9, NIV).

2. *Peace* reminds us of the traditional Hebrew greeting *Shalom,* which conveys the idea of total well-being. For the Christian, *peace* denotes a restored relationship with God and one's fellowman, made possible by divine reconciliation and forgiveness. *Peace* is the condition of inner rest with which Christ graces the life of the believer. Before He left His disciples Jesus bequeathed to them

peace: "Peace I leave with you; my peace I give to you; not as the world gives do I give to you. Let not your hearts be troubled, neither let them be afraid" (John 14:27, RSV).

3. In an exception to the usual salutation, Paul adds a passing reference to the work of Christ which makes possible our experience of grace and peace. He "gave himself for our sins to rescue us from the present evil age" (4, NIV). The active verb "gave" stresses Christ's voluntary gift of himself, and the reflexive pronoun "himself" emphasizes the totality of His surrender. Our sins put Him on the cross, but Calvary's suffering was effective, in that it "rescued" us from (took us out of) this present, transitory, evil age and gave us spiritual status in the new age of the Spirit. Emancipation from sin is the essential product of the Cross. With this note the Apostle lays down a challenge to the false missionaries who appear to be keeping the Galatian believers from living in the freedom of the new age.

4. All this occurs *according to the will of God and our Father.* He is the Author of the way of reconciliation and freedom. Let every believer join in the doxology: *To whom be glory forever and ever. Amen!* (5). The Epistle therefore begins with a call to give the glory to God and it ends with a condemnation of any glory in the flesh and a testimony of the Apostle that he is determined to glory only *in the cross of our Lord Jesus Christ, by whom the world is crucified unto me, and I unto the world* (6:12-14).

The Authenticity of Paul's Gospel

Galatians 1:6—2:21

No Other Gospel

Galatians 1:6-10

> 6 I marvel that ye are so soon removed from him that called you into the grace of Christ unto another gospel:
> 7 Which is not another; but there be some that trouble you, and would pervert the gospel of Christ.
> 8 But though we, or an angel from heaven, preach any other gospel unto you than that which we have preached unto you, let him be accursed.
> 9 As we said before, so say I now again, if any man preach any other gospel unto you than that ye have received, let him be accursed.
> 10 For do I now persuade men, or God? or do I seek to please men? for if I yet pleased men, I should not be the servant of Christ.

One is surprised that Paul does not follow his salutation with the usual word of gratitude for the loyalty to Christ and effective ministry of the readers. It becomes immediately obvious that he is hurting over the threatening apostasy of the churches. Ridderbos comments: "For an expression of interest in the fortunes and the struggle for those churches, this is not the place. The painful and dangerous alienation between the apostle and the churches must be discussed forthwith and headon."[1]

1. *The incredible right-about face* (6). Paul is aghast that the Galatians *are so soon removed from him that called* them and are turning to *another gospel*. At stake is the gospel itself. As we shall come to see, as we work through this majestic Epistle, the gospel, for Paul, is one of free grace. It is the good news that God accepts us not on the

basis of our good works but solely on the ground of our faith in Jesus Christ. A lifetime of meritorious deeds will not satisfy the demands of God's holiness, only trust in the work of Christ at Calvary. As Joachim Jeremias has so beautifully suggested, the only deed of merit acceptable to God is the death of Christ. By faith I grasp that Cross and hold it out to God.[2] Christ's deed alone will save us. For a Christian to begin to add anything to that act of faith as necessary for salvation is to destroy the gospel.

The Galatians are allowing themselves to be drawn away and what hurts Paul is that they are deserting not only him as the one who first proclaimed the truth to them but God himself who called them through Paul *into the grace of Christ*. More than ignorance is involved here; there is culpable action on their part. While temptation-filled oppression and subtle circumstances may figure significantly in one's backsliding, the person must bear the responsibility for failing to tap the resources of grace for instruction and spiritual strength.

2. *The one and only gospel* (7). In verse 6, Paul accuses them of deserting (like soldiers from an army, an almost unforgivable deed) the gospel for *another (heteros) gospel*. But then he says that the gospel of the Judaizers is not really *another (allos)* gospel (7). What is the difference? *Heteros* implies a difference of kind while *allos* implies addition. *Heteros* means "one of two," whereas *allos* means "one besides." In fact, *heteros* signifies "unlike" or "opposite."

Paul seems to imply in verse 6 that there can be two gospels, but that is out of keeping with the thrust of the passage. Rather he says, "It is not another gospel, for there cannot be two gospels, and as it is not the same, it is no gospel at all."[3] Perversion of the gospel in any degree is destruction of the gospel. To add anything to it by way of requirements other than faith is to turn the gospel into bad news. The Greek word for *pervert* in verse 7 literally means "reverse" or "change to the opposite." Only one hopeful word of salvation for mankind exists and it arises out of the redeeming work of Christ. All this reminds us of Peter's word to the religious leaders of Judaism: "There is salvation in no one else, for there is no other name under heaven given among men by which we must be saved" (Acts 4:12, RSV). Not even the name of Moses!

3. *The curse of modification* (8-9). Sinful men find it difficult to bring themselves under the authoritative truth of the gospel. Thus, the biggest temptation is to seek to modify it to conform to their human weaknesses. Paul asserts that even if he should fall into the error of preaching *any other gospel* than that which he had preached to the Galatians, or if one such as an angel with status in heaven should do the same, he would fall under the curse of God. All this simply means that the gospel equals grace and any salvation offered outside the gospel is salvation by works of the law, and in effect no gospel at all. Paul writes later, "All who rely on works of the law are under a curse; for it is written, 'Cursed be everyone who does not abide by all things written in the book of the law, and do them'" (3:10, RSV).

4. *The source of authority* (10). Whenever a serious theological or doctrinal issue develops in the life of the church, the matter of authority is always raised. What is the source of truth? To whom should we turn for answers? This is precisely the situation to which Paul addresses himself in this letter.

After instructing the Galatians to declare *accursed,* or "ban from the community," any person who is preaching a gospel contrary to the one they received, Paul attacks an apparent accusation that he was fashioning his gospel so as to curry favor with men (1:10). By no means would he "win converts" at any price. The Judaizers no doubt were sure that his alleged "freewheeling on grace" was a subtle means of gaining followers, to the expense of holy living. In response Paul makes it clear that all is done in service to Christ. "His personal popularity is the last thing he is concerned about, otherwise he would not be writing to the Galatians in such strong terms."[4] In effect, Paul wants it clearly understood he is guided by the gospel and by the commitment to servanthood to which it has called him. The gospel is his guide and authority, the final court of appeal in all things Christian. For us, confronted with heretical teaching, the Living Word, Christ, and the written Word, the Bible, constitute our authority.

By Special Revelation

Galatians 1:11-12

> 11 But I certify you, brethren, that the gospel which was preached of me is not after man.
> 12 For I neither received it of man, neither was I taught it, but by the revelation of Jesus Christ.

1. Sometimes, when a person speaks, we find ourselves wondering as to the origin of his ideas. Are they his own? Or has he appropriated the views of others? Paul must have been sensing that the Galatians were questioning his characterization of the Christian gospel. His answer is forthright: "The gospel you heard me preach is no human invention" (1:11, NEB). No human being could have conceived this plan of redemption which opened salvation to both Jew and Gentile. Indeed, not even Paul, this fanatically devoted Jew, could have thought it up. This gospel is not "man's gospel," that is, a humanistic attempt to bring hope to disillusioned mankind. Paul thus makes it abundantly clear that he did not receive the message he preaches from human sources.

2. Neither was he tutored in the faith and eventually came to accept it. The method by which he received his gospel was not by personal instruction, the way that the great majority of Christians before him received it. Burton comments: "As a pupil of the Pharisees he had been taught something very different from the gospel, but he had had no connection with those who at the beginning were the teachers of the gospel."[5] One must not assume, however,

that Paul had not heard something of the life and message of Christ, for more than once he refers to the contents of the gospel in the sense of it having been transmitted to him by the earliest followers of Jesus (see 1 Cor. 15:3-4). He obviously means that no teacher unfolded to him systematically the heart of the gospel, that which really makes the gospel the gospel, the good news of salvation for all.

3. Paul declares that the gospel he preached to the Galatians came by *the revelation of Jesus Christ* (12b). "Revelation" here means "a divine disclosure" or "a divine bringing-into-view." At a point in time, the Apostle perceived, through God's assistance, the truth which makes his gospel authentic. The phrase *the revelation of Jesus Christ* can refer either to Christ as the revealed One or to Christ as the Revealer. By the former, Paul would be affirming that Jesus Christ himself as Messiah has been revealed to him and in such a way that the disclosure carried with it the substance of the gospel. By the latter, he would be saying that Christ is the One who reveals the content of the gospel.

Based upon what Paul is about to say concerning his earlier Christian opposition to *the church of God* (13) and what we know from his writings concerning his later personal commitment to Christ, the first interpretation seems more proper. *The revelation of Jesus Christ* was divine insight into who Christ is. It carried with it the conviction that He is indeed the Son of God (see 1:16). The experience on the Damascus Road at once shattered Paul's stubborn hate for Christ and opened his heart and mind to perceive the true nature of Christ as Lord. Christ took hold of him (Phil. 3:12) and Paul, in turn, found himself questing to know Christ better and better (Phil. 3:7-10).

4. Two arresting Christian truths underlie this declaration. *(a)* Christ himself is the gospel, the good news. His presence, an expression of the divine love and mercy, is the hope of deliverance from the guilt and power of sin.

(b) Authority in ministry arises out of the unforgettable consciousness that one has been addressed by God and called into ministry. No person, be he ever so clever with words and ideas, can long survive the onslaughts of the adversary against his proclamation if deep in his soul there is lacking a pulsating assurance that God has given him *the good news* of all history to share with every needy sinner.

Attested in His Remarkable Experience

Galatians 1:13-24

13 For ye have heard of my conversation in time past in the Jews' religion, how that beyond measure I persecuted the church of God, and wasted it:

14 And profited in the Jews' religion above many my equals in mine own nation, being more exceedingly zealous of the traditions of my fathers.

15 But when it pleased God, who separated me from my mother's womb, and called me by his grace,

16 To reveal his Son in me, that I might preach him among the heathen; immediately I conferred not with flesh and blood:

17 Neither went I up to Jerusalem to them which were apostles before me; but I went into Arabia, and returned again unto Damascus.

18 Then after three years I went up to Jerusalem to see Peter, and abode with him fifteen days.

19 But other of the apostles saw I none, save James the Lord's brother.

20 Now the things which I write unto you, behold, before God, I lie not.

21 Afterwards I came into the regions of Syria and Cilicia;

22 And was unknown by face unto the churches of Judaea which were in Christ:

23 But they had heard only, That he which persecuted us in times past now preacheth the faith which once he destroyed.

24 And they glorified God in me.

Several points are made by the Apostle in further support of his contention that his gospel is indeed the true one and did not originate from association with, or instruction from, certain Christians.

1. *He exceeded others in his pre-Christian sectarianism and persecuting zeal* (13-14). He readily appeals to the facts of his pre-conversion, hostile life, which his readers apparently knew, perhaps from Paul's testimony which he shared with them while he was with them. His intense

hostility, issuing in a dogged persecution of the Christians, made him virtually impervious to the preaching and practice of the Christians. While God must have used the Christians to impact Paul's spirit in ways we cannot imagine, Paul feels that a special sovereign address by God brought him to an acceptance of Christ as his Savior.

Sectarian or cultic prejudice can spawn all kinds of rationalized injustices. Witness the stoning of Stephen! "Saul was consenting to his death" (Acts 8:1, RSV). Witness Paul's violent action against the Church! "Saul laid waste the church, and entering house after house, he dragged off men and women and committed them to prison" (Acts 8:3, RSV). All this maddening action was to the end of wiping out *the church of God* (13).

In what sense had Paul advanced beyond his fellow Jews (14)? In all likelihood he has in mind "the achievement of righteousness according to the standards and ideals of Pharisaism"[6] (see Phil. 3:5-6). This deeply ingrained works-righteousness played a significant part in generating his passion to defend Judaism against all heresy. He felt that the truths which had been passed on to him from his spiritual elders must be protected at any price.

Every social organization—academic, political, educational or religious—in its history develops peculiar beliefs, customs, and practices and their *traditions* can either foster continuing vitality or blind the eyes to changing responsibilities and lead to irrational actions to preserve the group at the tragic cost of losing its reason for existence. The history of the Christian Church is not without its soiled pages in this regard.

2. *Paul's independent apostleship is further attested by his action following his conversion* (15-17). He did not confer with *flesh and blood,* that is, with human leaders, especially the apostles or the followers of Christ (16b). But this point is preceded with another reference to the distinctiveness of his experience with God.

a. Like the prophets Jeremiah and John the Baptist, he believed he had been set apart to ministry before his birth (15).

b. He had been called *by his grace,* by which Paul means that nothing in his previous "righteous" life could have opened his heart to God and thus have led God to choose him for ministry. His sense of calling arose out of the revelation of divine love which finally brought him to realize that he was "favored" by God. It was all a gift of the love of God. To Paul, "the origin of all human salvation is in the mind and loving purpose of God."[7] But this does not obviate response on the part of a person. The Apostle made this necessity clear in his testimony to King Agrippa: "I was not disobedient unto the heavenly vision" (Acts 26:19).

c. The pleasure of God in this act was to reveal Christ to and through Paul, and that action in turn becomes the process of his ministry to the Gentiles (16a). Cole comments: "What begins by being a revelation of Christ to Paul becomes a revelation of Christ in Paul as the Spirit produces His fruits in unaccustomed soil. And as Paul preaches to the Gentiles the unsearchable riches of Christ, so Christ is revealed through him."[8] At its best, Christian preaching is a revelatory act; through words, freighted with the Spirit, Christ appears to needy men.

By a reiteration of the above facts, Paul hopes his readers would understand his sense of apostolic independence. His ministerial commission does not depend upon other human beings nor was it subject to their control. So there was no quick journey to Jerusalem following his conversion on the Damascus Road. We should not read arrogance into this statement. Apparently the Twelve had already established themselves as the leaders of the Church, and Jerusalem had become its principal center. However, Paul was so certain of the deity and messiahship of Christ and the call of God to minister to the Gentiles, he did not need the confirmation of the Christian leaders at Jerusalem.

Rather, Paul felt the absorbing need to commune with God, so he journeyed into Arabia. While it is enchanting to believe that the little Jew from Tarsus took off on an evangelistic trip to preach to the "barbarous and savage people" of Arabia, as the Early Church Fathers conjectured, more likely he simply sought communion with God. The revelation of Jesus as the Son of God so undermined the structure of Pharisaic thought, to which Paul had committed himself, it would take more than an hour or a day to build an entirely new system of belief.

Just think of the task before Paul! If there had been no intrinsic and historical relationship of Christ to the Old Testament faith, the effort would not have been so difficult, even for that clever and well-trained mind of Paul. But a radical revision of his old beliefs was demanded as a result of the placing of Christ at the heart of his faith. The sparsely inhabited region of Arabia, with all its rich history for his own people, provided just the setting for thinking through his new commitment to Christ. Great Christians listen carefully to teachers and leaders of the Church, but great Christians also have those lonely, learning trysts with the teaching Christ.

3. *Paul's gospel is effective even though it does not depend upon the approval of the Jerusalem leaders.* This fact also attests its authenticity (18-24). Being the honest person he is, Paul quickly acknowledges the importance of the teaching of the apostles. He admits that, after three years, he went up to Jerusalem, where he spent two weeks visiting with Peter (18) and on one occasion met James, the Lord's brother (19 cf. Acts 9:19b-31). But by that time, his message was crystalized. His visit carried no official purpose; for sure, it was not intended to give him special instruction. The original language suggests that he desired only to make the acquaintance of the church leaders. In no way could his gospel, therefore, be owed to the Jerusalem church. Paul's relationship to the apostolic circle there-

fore was extremely limited. The opposition Paul sustained may have been coming from persons who were appealing to the authority of Peter and James.

Furthermore, in support of his argument Paul states that the next phase of his post-conversion experience after Arabia, Damascus, and Jerusalem was far away and out of the reach of Jerusalem (21). He went into *the regions of Syria and Cilicia.* These areas were near his hometown. Acts 9:30 records that he left Jerusalem and went to Tarsus via Caesarea, the port city of Palestine at that time. The result of this withdrawal to the north was that he remained *unknown by face* (personally) *unto the churches of Judaea* (22). However, the report out of Jerusalem was that those very churches rejoiced over the fact that the one who formerly persecuted them was now preaching the gospel which he once tried to destroy (23-24). Paul virtually demolishes the argument of his opponents who possibly derived their impetus from these Judean churches. Paul reminds them that these Judean churches originally acknowledged that he was preaching the truth. He quotes verbatim what they were saying about him: "Our former persecutor is now preaching the faith which he once tried to destroy" (23). Paul's conversion was considered by them to have been genuine, to have been God's work, and they praised God for it (24).

The message validates the messenger. The Judean churches were convinced of the turnabout in Paul's life, not just because he no longer persecuted them but mainly because he was faithfully preaching the gospel. The opponents of Paul were thus condemned, in the mind of Paul, for assuming an error in his gospel of freedom from a legalistic, works-oriented religion. The final answer to their charges was that his message had its source in a divine revelation and not in human concepts. William McCumber is correct when he insists that "a preacher's credibility is the integrity of his message." Christians in our day must take time to scrutinize the messages emanating, in almost baffling confusion, from the airwaves.

Do they rest upon the written Word? Do they send forth a clear call to repentance and faith? Do they promise a life of righteousness and holiness through the power of the indwelling Holy Spirit?

GALATIANS 2

Vindicated Finally by the Jerusalem Leaders

Galatians 2:1-10

> 1 Then fourteen years after I went up again to Jerusalem with Barnabas, and took Titus with me also.
> 2 And I went up by revelation, and communicated unto them that gospel which I preach among the Gentiles, but privately to them which were of reputation, lest by any means I should run, or had run, in vain.
> 3 But neither Titus, who was with me, being a Greek, was compelled to be circumcised:
> 4 And that because of false brethren unawares brought in, who came in privily to spy out our liberty which we have in Christ Jesus, that they might bring us into bondage:
> 5 To whom we gave place by subjection, no, not for an hour; that the truth of the gospel might continue with you.
> 6 But of these who seemed to be somewhat, (whatsoever they were, it maketh no matter to me: God accepteth no man's person:) for they who seemed to be somewhat in conference added nothing to me:
> 7 But contrariwise, when they saw that the gospel of the uncircumcision was committed unto me, as the gospel of the circumcision was unto Peter;
> 8 (For he that wrought effectually in Peter to the apostleship of the circumcision, the same was mighty in me toward the Gentiles:)
> 9 And when James, Cephas, and John, who seemed to be pillars, perceived the grace that was given unto me, they gave to me and Barnabas the right hands of fellowship; that we should go unto the heathen, and they unto the circumcision.
> 10 Only they would that we should remember the poor; the same which I also was forward to do.

Paul understood that he had to demonstrate conclusively that his message to the Gentiles was not out of harmony with that of the mother church in Jerusalem. This he attempts to do in these 10 verses.

1. The visit *fourteen years after* (1). We encounter here one of the most complicated problems of New Testament

study. Which visit to Jerusalem recorded in the Book of Acts corresponds with the description given here? Also, does Paul mean 14 years after his first visit to Jerusalem or 14 years after his conversion? The Book of Acts describes three visits of Paul to Jerusalem: 9:26, following his escape from Damascus; 11:30, taking assistance to the church at the time of the famine; 15:2, conferring with the church leaders at the Council of Jerusalem. The adverb *again* (2:1) might mean a second visit or possibly a third or any subsequent visit.

The fact that Paul does not refer specifically in Galatians 2 to the decisions of the Council of Jerusalem would support the view that the visit to Jerusalem is to be identified with an earlier trip, likely at the time of the famine (Acts 11:30). If this is correct, Paul and Barnabas took the opportunity afforded by this famine-visit to have an interview with the leaders of the Jerusalem church. Moreover, the *fourteen years* probably should be related to his conversion, reckoned to have occurred in A.D. 33. So this visit can be dated about A.D. 46.

Whatever conclusions one might reach on these technical problems of chronology, the chief point for Paul is that a very considerable lapse of time transpired between the beginning of his ministry and this dialogue with the leaders. As Cole concludes, "Paul has already engaged in the Gentile mission for some years and there is no question about the gospel he preaches being fully developed."[9] By this time Paul had evangelized in Syria and Cilicia (1:21) and at Tarsus (Acts 9:30; 11:25). He certainly does not need to seek their permission now.

2. *By revelation* (2). Paul is not pressured by his enemies to make the trip to Jerusalem. They would have gleefully pounced on any admission on the part of Paul that he was capitulating to the Jerusalem authorities. He says he has divine direction to go. We do not know the method by which this revelation came, but this much is certain, Paul received it in true spiritual openness and submission. Despite all the theories of critics concerning the doctrinal

and ethical struggles in the early years, the Church seems always ready to listen to the Spirit's direction in the resolution of them.

3. "Those who were of repute" (2, 6, RSV). Upon arrival in Jerusalem, privately Paul *communicated,* ("declared," "laid out for consideration") *to them which were of reputation* the gospel which he had been preaching. In verse 9 Paul tells us who these influential men were: James, Peter and John. They were the pillars of the mother church of Christendom. Two of them, Peter, and John the son of Zebedee, were prominent apostles, and the other, James, was the brother of Jesus. These three men had by this time proven themselves to be dependable and stable interpreters of Christ and faithful pastors of the people.

Verse 6 raises some questions as to Paul's attitude toward these men: "From those who were reputed to be something (what they were makes no difference to me; God shows no partiality)—those, I say, who were of repute added nothing to me" (RSV). At this point one receives the impression of a crescendo of resentment on the part of Paul over the way in which the Judaizers are contrasting his authority with that of the Jerusalem leaders. Apparently, his opponents were saying, "Because these men were with Christ in His ministry, their opinions on matters of doctrine and church life must be respected above those of an outsider like Paul." But to the apostle Paul (who, incidentally, does not refer to these leaders as apostles), their authority does not rest solely upon their knowledge of the earthly Jesus. Rather, the inward acceptance of Christ as Messiah and Lord upon His revelation of himself to a person, as was the case with Paul, carried a complementary and more important authority.

In response to this unfair, external struggle, Paul makes two points. First, "What they were makes no difference to me" (6, RSV), that is, though these men were once related to Christ historically, that did not seem to be important to Christ when He called Paul to a special apostleship. Thus one should not accord to them special status because of the historical association. Second, *God accepteth no man's person* (6); that is, "God is not influenced by outward circumstances, such as rank, wealth, or position within the church."[10] All this means essentially that the theological issue is of such magnitude that one must not be unduly influenced by ecclesiastical status. However, it is "proper to render judgment upon the existing status of people, past or present while applying the rule of God's impartiality."[11]

4. "I took Titus along" (1, NIV). The introduction of the word about Titus is not to be taken as a passing historical note. Titus is presented as evidence that Paul had not *run in vain,* that is, Paul's gospel has validity and power (2). Titus was a Greek, an uncircumcised Christian, and the Apostle has taken him along as "a living piece of evidence" that the gospel is effective in transforming the lives of the Gentiles. Verse 3, in the Greek, reads literally, "But not even Titus . . . was compelled to be circumcised." In other words, Titus was put to the test by the leaders in Jerusalem but was not forced by them to submit to circumcision (see 5:1-12; 6:12-16), this passé sign of the old covenant. He proved to be fully acceptable as a member of the Christian church. Thus, if Titus can be accepted, then the principle holds that all Gentiles can be received into the fellowship without submission to the Jewish law, as the antipauline preachers were insisting.

5. *False brethren unawares brought in* (4). Who were these *false brethren?* Quite obviously Paul is referring to his Jewish Christian opponents at Jerusalem. The term *false brethren* expresses his judgment of their interpretation of the gospel. They evidently think of themselves as orthodox and devoted Christians and are fighting to preserve the faith as they understand it. But for Paul they are "pseudo-Christians" because they deny that the Gentile Christians can be saved by God's grace alone (2:21). The issue is clear. In the minds of these *false brethren* the Gentile must first become a Jew before he can be considered a Christian.

What is most reprehensible for Paul is that these men were "secretly brought in . . . to spy out our freedom" (4, RSV). Military language is now employed by Paul to demonstrate the insidious nature of the struggle. Like undercover agents or conspirators they were brought in to bring this situation, and especially Paul and his disciples, under control. Their intention was to *bring us into bondage* (4).

The Greek does not help us to decide whether they are "smuggled in" or "sneaked in." If "brought in" is the proper translation, the agitators may have come from the Galatia region and are introduced into the church by some such group as the Pharisaic party mentioned in Acts 15:5 who are zealous for the law. "Sneaked in" may simply mean that over a period of time the church had permitted some persons who were persuaded of the false gospel to continue in her fellowship.

The outcome of the encounter is that Paul stands firm under pressure and refuses to submit to these saboteurs on the solid ground that these men are insincere and that the truth of the gospel must be preserved at any cost (5).

6. *The gospel of the uncircumcision* (6-8). Nothing is said in this account about the debates which must have prevailed nor the nature of the arguments. Only the results are listed. (a) The people *who seemed to be somewhat* (6) add nothing to Paul's interpretation of the gospel. The point that matters is that these "men of high reputation" (NEB) are completely satisfied with Paul's account of his teachings and activities. (b) A division of missionary territory is agreed upon, Paul to be the apostle to the Gentiles, the uncircumcised, and Peter to be the apostle to the Jews, the circumcised. This means that the area where the Galatian churches existed is Pauline territory, and his proclamation of the gospel and its application to the church should prevail. (c) A complimentary word is spoken about Peter (8). As we shall come to see, a struggle develops between Peter and Paul (2:11 ff) but here (written

later) Paul acknowledges the effectiveness of Peter's ministry to his own people.

7. *The right hands of fellowship* (9). The conclusion of this affair was a full and glad recognition that the gospel preached by both the Mother Church and the Pauline churches was the same and they all were striving for the same end, the salvation of all men. This sense of unity or "belongingness" was sealed by extending *the right hands of fellowship,* a sign of friendship and trust.

Cole comments that this action on the part of the church leaders in Jerusalem must have been "a bitter blow" to the Judaizers. The heavier blow was to follow. For if Paul's gospel was accepted, then his apostleship must be accepted too."[12] James, Peter, and John *perceived the grace that was given to me* (9). The handclasp also was the acknowledgment of the territorial division mentioned above. The message thus went out to the Galatians that they should no longer listen to the specious lies of the Judaizers. "Paul's apostleship bore all the marks of a God-given authority; Peter and the others had accepted it."[13]

8. *Remember the poor* (10). The reference to remembering the poor is not to be taken as a general exhortation resting upon all good Jews or Christians but to a special provision of material assistance to the saints of Jerusalem who were suffering at this time. This is the only request laid upon Paul by the Jerusalem leaders. Paul is eager to respond to it and he does faithfully throughout his missionary career (see Acts 24:17; Rom. 15:25 ff; 1 Cor. 16:1 ff; 2 Corinthians 8—9).

Several concluding thoughts seem appropriate. First, "independence is a virtue—up to a point" (Blackwood). Paul possessed a great deal of it, but he also was committed to the Christian community. Thus, he was willing to engage in open discussion with the leaders over the issues which had developed between the Judaizers and himself. True community provides the basis for authentic freedom. Second, what does one do when men of repute in the church question your servanthood? *(a)* Lay the truth before them. *(b)* Make the aim of your life the preservation of the gospel above all. *(c)* Seek always to maintain the fellowship. *(d)* Be sensitive to the needs of the entire community.

Consistency in Witness

Galatians 2:11-13

> 11 But when Peter was come to Antioch, I withstood him to the face, because he was to be blamed.
> 12 For before that certain came from James, he did eat with the Gentiles: but when they were come, he withdrew and separated himself, fearing them which were of the circumcision.
> 13 And the other Jews dissembled likewise with him; insomuch that Barnabas also was carried away with their dissimulation.

We have just closed a section of the Epistle which has a happy ending. Paul and the church leaders in Jerusalem have come to a general agreement and a mutual acceptance of one another's role in the spreading of the gospel. Peter's specific task is to proclaim the Word to the Jews and Paul's is to go to the Gentiles, and "no one should refuse recognition of another's God-entrusted work."[14] But regretfully this commitment breaks down when Peter visits the church in Antioch.

No reason is given as to why Peter went to Antioch. It could have been one of his occasional visits, or perhaps a stopover on the way to some other place. We have good evidence from the biblical record (Acts 11:19-27; 14:26; 15:22, 30; 18:22) and Jewish sources that there was considerable travel by preachers between Jerusalem and Antioch. Also, Peter moved around the Mediterranean world following his ministry in Judea. It has been suggested that this appearance of Peter may have been a final move of the Church's center from Jerusalem to Antioch due to developing conflicts in Jerusalem with the authorities.

Antioch in Syria was a city heavily Greek in spirit and culture and was noted for its open way of life. There is every reason to believe that the Jews who had migrated from Palestine to this Syrian city in the first and second centuries before the Christian era had been attracted by its Hellenism. The church in Antioch had come into being under auspicious circumstances and could boast of a group of outstanding leaders (see Acts 11:19-24; 13:1-3). A free and tolerant spirit prevailed among these men and when Peter dropped in, he fell in line with it and had unrestrained table-fellowship with both Jews and Gentiles: *For before that certain came from James, he did eat with the Gentiles* (12a).

1. *Vacillation and compromise* (11-12). Quite obviously Peter, while a product of Jewish Christianity as it developed in the Jerusalem community, had been experiencing some changes in his attitude toward the Gentiles. The Cornelius experience, no doubt, had profound effect on him. When he came to Antioch, he "crossed the line" from the Jewish life based on the Law, as interpreted in those days by the rabbis, to an open relationship with these Gentile Christians who did not feel the need to come under the restrictions of the Law. The Law did not forbid the eating with the Gentiles but it had become traditional practice among orthodox Jews to abstain in order to avoid any risk of eating "unclean food." Peter's actions however, are in keeping with the spirit of the previous consultation in Jerusalem. There had been some handshaking on this matter; Jew and Gentile are understood to be one in Christ (2:9). But when *certain* (persons) *came from James,* the leader of the Jerusalem church at this time, Peter *withdrew and separated himself* (12) from the Gentiles.

Who are these "certain ones from James"? Are they the *false brethren* of 2:4-5? Probably not, for the false brethren did not approve of the agreements in Jerusalem. Were these persons instructed by James? That is a difficult question, and any answer would be conjecture. The result of the action of these men is reprehensible in the eyes of Paul. The shift in position by Peter greatly disturbs Paul, naturally, since he feels so keenly that the Church must be one. Beyond that is the fact that he and Barnabas, both Jews, had adopted this way of life with the Gentiles. He and Barnabas are thus repudiated. Moreover, as Betz suggests, the shift of Peter "must have become one of the preconditions for the Galatians' own plans to shift" from the gospel preached by Paul to that of the Judaizers (see 1:6-7).[15]

Paul concludes that Peter "stood condemned" (11, RSV) for his behavior, and so he has an open confrontation with him *(withstood him to the face)*. This is strong language, taken from military or political practice and usually employed in referring to the exposure of political or military infidelity of defection. Paul sees all of this as compromise but for Peter it may represent his failure to relate the unity principle with his natural respect for the legacy of the Old Testament faith. In verse 12 Paul writes that Peter *withdrew and separated himself.* Here is a possible play on words: "He separated himself," literally "He cut himself off," which may be Paul's way of saying "He played the Pharisee." The Pharisees prided themselves in being "the separated ones" who were anxious to preserve their cultic purity.

All of us who take seriously the responsibility of understanding our faith and of applying it faithfully to life know full well that consistency is difficult. Paul is pleading for consistency, which he apparently feels could be easily achieved. But maybe he fails to comprehend in this instance that the Big Fisherman is struggling to "put it all together." Peter vacillates, to be sure, but from his point of view it may be only a difference over nonessentials. William Neil concludes that Paul "could not have challenged Peter openly as he did had he not been sure that basically Peter and he were of one heart and mind on the matter. What he was objecting to was Peter's temporary agreement for reasons of expediency with a policy in which neither he nor Paul believed."[16]

2. *The effect of the dispute* (13). Paul comments that the *other Jews dissembled likewise with him; insomuch that Barnabas also was carried away with their dissimulation* (13). Peter manages to get the Jews who are part of that church to join him in the withdrawal. The verb *dissembled* means literally "playacted", that is, "acted hypocritically." *Dissimulation* means "hypocrisy." Paul obviously feels that Peter manipulates these Jews and thus they are to be classed with him as hypocrites. This is Paul's evaluation. The Jews probably have arrived at the same conclusion for themselves and should not be accused of moral and spiritual corruption.

What hurt Paul deeply was the fact that Barnabas, his dear friend and early teacher, was compelled to go along with *the other Jews.* Barnabas *also was carried away* by them. Betz comments that this verb suggests a certain irrationality in the act of Barnabas, this is to say, he was *carried away* emotionally. We really cannot say why Barnabas joined the anti-Pauline group. Apparently, he was something of a victim of the struggle. Betz writes: "The fact that a man like Barnabas decided against his former student and fellow worker shows how difficult a question the Antioch meeting had to decide."[17] When we view the statement in Acts 15:36-40 as to the breakup of Paul and Barnabas over taking Mark on the second missionary journey, we wonder if maybe the ties between them had not been loosened over this earlier issue.

It is difficult to deal constructively with this Antioch episode. One would hesitate to condemn either of these men; both were such staunch disciples of our Lord and contributors to the establishment and growth of the Early Church. It is not for us to be critical, for, as one has written, we have enough persons in the Christian community today who are censorious. To repeat, independence is a virtue—up to a point. But when it begins to divide the body of believers, serious attention must be given to developing means of open dialogue about the issues involved. Paul really tried to do that with the Jerusalem leaders. He thought a sound agreement had been reached and when Peter acted as he did, Paul was deeply disturbed, and rightly so.

Andrew Blackwood comments that "the distinctive curse of Protestantism has been divisiveness, unwillingness to consider the other person a Christian because of some real or fancied disagreement."[18]

Grace Means Freedom

Galatians 2:14-21

> 14 But when I saw that they walked not uprightly according to the truth of the gospel, I said unto Peter before them all, If thou, being a Jew, livest after the manner of Gentiles, and not as do the Jews, why compellest thou the Gentiles to live as do the Jews?
> 15 We who are Jews by nature, and not sinners of the Gentiles,
> 16 Knowing that a man is not justified by the works of the law, but by the faith of Jesus Christ, even we have believed in Jesus Christ, that we might be justified by the faith of Christ, and not by the works of the law: for by the works of the law shall no flesh be justified.
> 17 But if, while we seek to be justified by Christ, we ourselves also are found sinners, is therefore Christ the minister of sin? God forbid.
> 18 For if I build again the things which I destroyed, I make myself a transgressor.
> 19 For I through the law am dead to the law, that I might live unto God.
> 20 I am crucified with Christ: nevertheless I live; yet not I, but Christ liveth in me: and the life which I now live in the flesh I live by the faith of the Son of God, who loved me, and gave himself for me.
> 21 I do not frustrate the grace of God: for if righteousness come by the law, then Christ is dead in vain.

Paul now launches into the reasons why he must confront Peter and his Jewish friends with the issue of their conduct with regard to table fellowship with the Gentiles. *They walked not uprightly according to the truth of the gospel* (14). The *New English Bible* reads: "Their conduct did not square with the truth of the Gospel." The issue is indeed the relationship between belief and conduct, and Paul is calling for that which is consistent with the truth of the gospel. Interestingly, the Greek word translated *walked . . . uprightly* is the one from which we get "orthodoxy." Literally, it means "go straight toward a goal" or "proceed on the right road." In this case, these persons are acting in an unorthodox manner; they are not proceeding on the road which the gospel had set out for them. They are no longer under the control of the gospel (see 1:6-7).

1. *The ultimate contradiction of the faith.* In the presence of all the people, perhaps in an assembly much like the Jerusalem meeting, Paul asks Peter: "If you, though a Jew, live like a Gentile and not like a Jew, how can you compel the Gentiles to live like Jews?" (14, RSV). The logic of Paul is cutting. Paul flatly declares that Peter, though by birth a Jew, no longer is living (present tense) as a Jew, that is to say, he is not conducting himself according to the religious life-style required of a Jew. He is not keeping the Jewish customs and laws. Rather, he is living *after the manner of Gentiles.* The use of the present tense, Betz avers, implies more than dining with Gentile Christians. It suggests that sharing the non-kosher menu of the Gentiles is the only external symbol of Peter's total emancipation from Judaism.[19] Thus, the sudden withdrawal is a self-contradiction. How could Peter now require the Gentiles to live like Jews? The obvious answer is, of course, negative. His own behavior nullifies that requisite. In English, if we were addressing Peter, we probably would have said something like this: "If your convictions permit you to act freely so as to live in a Gentile life-style, why do you insist that the Gentiles live only according to the Jewish life-style? Why do you not grant them the same freedom you enjoy?" Or, "You have been delivered from the customs and laws of Judaism, why don't you permit them to live out their newfound lives under Christ, free from the bondage of the Jewish religious code?"

Betz' conclusion is incisive:

> Ironically, therefore, by attempting to preserve the integrity of the Jewish Christians as Jews, Cephas destroys the integrity of the Gentile Christians as believers in Christ. Instead of welcoming them as converts to Christianity, he wants to make them into converts of Judaism. This contradicts the principles of the doctrine by faith, which had been the basis of the faith thus far (see 2:15-16).[20]

The problem may reflect what Peter and the Judaizers really were thinking about the character of the faith of the Gentiles. It would appear that withdrawal from table fellowship implied that the Gentile Christians are not as good as the Jewish Christians. Something is lacking in their faith and life. Why separate, if this is not true? Action in this case speaks louder than words. Ultimately, a contradiction is uncovered and Paul knows it.

What about the Lord's Supper? Would these Jewish Christians meet with the Gentile Christians for that meal? Whenever we refuse to participate in the Lord's Supper, baptism, or worship with others who claim to know our Lord in His forgiveness and cleansing, we certainly do strongly imply that we possess something they do not possess. We deny them full status as Christians. If a common faith in Christ does not bring us together, there must be an inherent contradiction somewhere.

2. *Saved by faith* (15-21). The remaining portion of this chapter contains a very closely reasoned argument by the Apostle in support of his plea for spiritual freedom for the Gentiles. One has to ask, Where does the dispute with Peter end and the theological reflection begin? No precise point of shift is discernible. Paul gets caught up in the experiential meaning of this episode and probably is unaware of the change himself. Life and doctrine flow together inseparably for him. The argument is directed essentially to the Jewish Christians and Peter. He must convince them, by reference to the experience of the salvation they are now enjoying, that what has just transpired is out of keeping with that experience.

a. Paul begins with the declaration of the universal commitment of all so-called Christian Jews to the truth that justification comes by faith (15-16). He ropes in all the Jewish Christians—Peter, the other Jews, and even the Judaizers—reminding them of their common human and spiritual heritage: *we who are Jews by nature, and not sinners of the Gentiles* (15). They all are separate from the

Gentiles by birth. This is the evidence of Jewishness. Moreover, they are not *sinners of the Gentiles,* or, "sinners from [the] Gentiles." Historically, the Gentiles did not have the privileges of forgiveness accorded the Jews through the old covenant cultic offerings. So, in effect, Paul is saying, "In talking about this matter of salvation, let's just talk about the relationship of us Jews to the gospel."

While the Jews had the law, they did not enjoy acceptance with God. They did not experience "justification by their works" of the law. They discovered that it is *by the faith of Jesus Christ,* or, "through faith in Jesus Christ" (RSV) that a person is justified. It was for that reason that Paul, and even the Judaizers, *believed in Jesus Christ.* It was through faith in Jesus that their lives were transformed and they realized finally their acceptance with God.

The logic of Paul's argument is sound. In effect, he says to his opponents, "By believing on Christ, you not only confessed that law-keeping is ineffectual in commending one to God, but also declared that faith in Christ is the only basis for that commendation. Righteousness is by faith in Jesus the Messiah and not by faith in the Law." As Cole states, "The present insistence of the Judaizers on the keeping of the law is utterly at variance with their own basic attitude."[21] And to clinch his point Paul paraphrases a word from Ps. 143:2: *for by the works of the law shall no flesh be justified* (16).

b. Justified is a key word in this passage. It comes from a root meaning "to make right," "to declare right," "to acquit." The concept is a metaphor from the courtroom. When a person, who has been charged with a crime which he has not committed, is brought into court, the jury examines the evidence and finally comes to the decision that the person is innocent. The judge then renders a decision of acquittal and the person goes free. He is declared innocent, and his citizenship remains intact. But there is a significant difference with the Christian who has been justified. He was indeed a wrongdoer, according to the laws of God. However, the Divine Judge, in compassion for the sinner, sent His Son to suffer on the Cross in behalf of the sinner, and thereby He can declare and make righteous the sinner who accepts in faith the meritorious work of the Son at Calvary in his behalf. To be justified really means to be pronounced and treated as righteous, and thereby to become righteous or receive the gift of righteousness. As one has suggested, to be justified means to be right-wised with God, and to continue to live in that relationship. Justification comes not by human moral achievement, therefore, but by a divine gift upon the response of faith. That is the meaning of grace.

c. Paul further declares the nature of the freedom which grace brings to the believing person.

(1) *It is the freedom of "being" rather than of "doing."* Verses 17-19 carry this inference. Behind them rests the dichotomy of the law-way of righteousness and the grace-way of righteousness, or the works-way of righteousness and the faith-way of righteousness. Judaism preached the first way, and Christians the second way. Paul saw Peter and the Judaizers falling back into the first way of experiencing the righteousness or salvation of God, and he determined to hold tenaciously to the second teaching. He believed firmly that freedom was possible only through faith (see Phil. 3:1-11). If one through the mere performance of good deeds as demanded by the Law sought acceptance with God, he would find only frustration and bondage (5:1-4). In Rom. 8:2-3 Paul writes: "The law of the Spirit of life in Christ Jesus has set me free from the law of sin and death. For God has done what the law, weakened by the flesh, could not do: sending his own Son in the likeness of sinful flesh and for sin, he condemned sin in the flesh, in order that the just requirement of the law might be fulfilled in us, who walk not according to the flesh but according to the Spirit" (RSV). It is the becoming a new person through faith in the atoning work of Christ that

enables the Christian to be free before God and to live out the requirements of God's law.

On the basis of this teaching of the relation of faith to works, Paul knew that his hearers would accuse him of removing all incentive to moral effort. This possibility is what lies behind verses 17 and 18. Paul believes that the faith-way bears in itself all the needed moral urgency, so that a person does indeed strive through the power of new life in faith to conduct himself in accordance with the will of God. Cole paraphrases verse 17 in this manner: "If, at the very moment while we say that we ourselves are justified by faith alone, we turn out to be preaching to others that 'faith alone' is inadequate, but that they must keep the law as well, does that not mean that trusting in Christ is only leading them into sin? for it is teaching them not to trust the law."[22] Verse 18 is a follow-up on this idea. *If I build again the things which I destroyed, I make myself a transgressor* (18). The Judaizers, with their insistence on this legalistic view of redemption, were building up the works-way of righteousness again, a total denial of the gift of salvation which comes by faith in Christ. All the law could ever do is to enable a person to show that he is a law-breaker and needs God's help (see 3:19-25).

A Christian enjoys the freedom of "being in Christ," something his life of human, moral effort never could give him. "Doing" for him is not the way of freedom; rather "being in Christ," that is, having the life of Christ within, is his liberty. Christ has brought about a death to the Law; or, to state it another way, through the power of faith the Law died in him, the law-way of seeking God's acceptance perished. Now he is "alive unto God" (19). Paul acknowledges that the Law as a schoolmaster also played a significant part in his quest for acceptance with God, for it taught him to see his moral and spiritual failure. He writes, "I through the law died to the law, that I might live to God" (19, RSV, see 3:24-26).

It must be kept in mind that Paul is not meaning to abandon the teaching of God as given in the Law of Moses;

rather, he means to say that he is no longer preaching that "doing the deeds of the law" will bring acceptance with God. Good works, however, now flow from the saved life because of the empowering life of Christ within (see Eph. 2:8-10).

(2) *It is the freedom of self-surrender instead of self-serving.* "I have been crucified with Christ; it is no longer I who live, but Christ who lives in me; and the life I now live in the flesh I live by faith in the Son of God, who loved me and gave himself for me" (2:20, RSV). The full extent of the relationship Paul now has with Christ is expressed in this verse. He has been crucified with Christ, that is, he has entered into Christ's death by faith and thus has died to sin. The power of sin has been broken in his life. Moreover, he has been resurrected with Christ into a new life. Richard Howard writes: "Death to sin is significant only because it makes the new life possible. Deliverance from sin is the opening of the door to a glorious new life in Christ."[23]

This new life is expressed in a striking way in the original language: "I live, no longer I *(ego),* but lives in me, Christ." Howard comments that the emphatic pronoun "ego" could be taken as simply emphasizing the personal aspect of the statement and be translated, "and I *myself* no longer live." However, the inclusion of the clause, *but Christ liveth in me,* seems to suggest that Paul is saying, "I live no longer *as I once did,* but in a new way— *no longer I.* Now Christ lives in me—He is the Lord of my new life."[24] A surrender of the full self to Christ has taken place in a crisis capitulation.

While the believer is delivered from the life of sinning, he still is under the domination of self, because of the Adamic sin. He must come to a new moment of yielding all his being unto God and only then can he be fully free. See the commands of Paul in Rom. 6:13, 19 and 12:1.

This new life of freedom is lived in the *flesh,* that is, in the present earthly body with all its limitations, temptations, and weaknesses but it is lived *by faith,* that is, by continued trust and obedient response to the Spirit of Christ. It is also lived with a prevailing consciousness of the price paid by Christ to purchase this new spiritual existence: *who gave himself* (at Calvary) *for me.* The man of faith can no longer live to serve his own self-centered ends. A full surrender to Christ sets him free to serve his Lord as a love slave.

(3) *It is the freedom of releasing instead of restricting the grace of God.* As Paul puts it, *I do not frustrate the grace of God: for if righteousness came by the law, then Christ is dead in vain* (21). He really is saying he does not "nullify" (RSV) or "render inept" the grace of God by the way he ministers and lives out his Christian commitment. He gets out of the way and lets God's love work in the hearts of men as he preaches and teaches. Grace means that God favors with forgiveness, newness of life, and cleansing all who come to Him by faith in Christ. It was true in Paul's personal experience and life and he knew it would be true for the Jews and the Gentiles if no restrictions, such as the demand to submit to circumcision, were thrown up against it. The tragedy of the struggle at Antioch was the raising of just such barriers. Paul would have nothing to do with it and he made that very plain. He wanted God to have freedom to do His saving work. He pleads for continued release of the divine grace in the hearts of his readers and in their churches.

Moreover, he saw the theological fallacy of any retreat to the law-way of justification. It announces to all men that the death of Christ was without purpose. Compared to the trivial requirements of the Law as a means of getting right with God, the Cross was, and is, the supreme miracle of God's love. Calvary is a constant reminder of the overwhelming love of God. God demonstrated His love at Calvary for us while we were yet sinners, struggling to save ourselves by our own humanly created good works (Rom. 5:8). Christianity is a religion of grace, which means that God has taken the initiative to redeem us from sin, to indwell us with His Spirit in order to make us what

He intended us to be. To take away the Cross is to nullify this grace, which in turn, is to take away the hope of salvation or spiritual freedom.

The Proof of History
Galatians 3:1—4:31

The Spirit as a Gift of Faith

Galatians 3:1-5

> 1 O foolish Galatians, who hath bewitched you, that ye should not obey the truth, before whose eyes Jesus Christ hath been evidently set forth, crucified among you?
> 2 This only would I learn of you, Received ye the Spirit by the works of the law, or by the hearing of faith?
> 3 Are ye so foolish? having begun in the Spirit, are ye now made perfect by the flesh?
> 4 Have ye suffered so many things in vain? if it be yet in vain.
> 5 He therefore that ministereth to you the Spirit, and worketh miracles among you, doeth he it by the works of the law, or by the hearing of faith?

Paul has been so taken up with the Antioch episode and with a testimony to his own deep experience of justification by grace through faith, he has lost sight of, for a moment, the people to whom he is writing. Here at the beginning of chapter 3 he returns to the experience of the Galatians and in a series of questions focuses on what occurred in their lives, not as a result of their devotion to the Law but by their faith in Christ. No doubt he remembers with clarity his campaign among them and how the living power of Christ so radically transformed their once-paganized lives. But now they are willing to listen to misinformed missionaries who are urging them to submit to the Law of Moses. Paul bursts out in "affectionate exasperation: You crazy people! You must be out of your minds!"[1]

Some kind of "black magic" must have been played on them, for Paul suggests that they have been *bewitched* (1), perhaps by an arch-Judaizer (2:12). This seems incredible to Paul, since before their very eyes "Jesus Christ was publicly portrayed as crucified" (3:1, RSV). Presumably this refers to the content of Paul's preaching when he evangelized them. He preached "Christ and him crucified" (1 Cor. 2:2). The Greek word *proegraphe* (1) bears the idea of placarding something in public, much like the huge signboards which clutter the sides of our highways. How could these Galatians have missed the meaning of the cross of Jesus Christ, the long-awaited Messiah of the Hebrews, whose death was endured to bring to an end the legalistic way of salvation.

Paul's argument proceeds along three lines.

1. *Received ye the Spirit by the works of the law, or by the hearing of faith?* (2). In effect, Paul is asking, "Tell me, at the beginning how did you become Christians? How did you receive the transforming Spirit?" The answer is obvious. Being Gentiles, they had not been living under the Law at the time of their conversion. They became Christians not by doing the works of the Law, not by doing morally acceptable good deeds, but on the basis of a response in faith to the gospel. If faith was sufficient for the reception of the Spirit then, why is it not sufficient now, in the ongoing of their Christian lives?

We Christians need frequent reminders of the unchanging truth that faith, and faith alone, is the condition for acceptance with God. But faith means for us to trust in God's Word and to render immediate obedience to it. When obedience is present and consistent, the deeds of the life of the believer will be brought into alignment with the eternal law of God.

What makes us Christians is the grace of God—a *spiritual* thing. What changes our lives to bring them into conformity with the nature and will of God is the indwelling power of God's Spirit. *Material* things, like circumcision and a regulated diet, cannot do it. They are not of the essence of the Christian life. Even our desperate efforts at goodness cannot create the Christian life. As Bonhoeffer once wrote, "Even our good intentions are not sufficient to bring us to the life in Christ."

2. *Having begun in the Spirit, are ye now made perfect by the flesh?* (3). "Spirit" and "flesh" are moral opposites in the thought of Paul (see Rom. 8: 5-9, RSV). By "flesh" he is not referring to our essential humanity; rather, he is defining human nature under the domination of sin. A person who is living "according to the flesh" is really living out of his own moral resources, which are very meager and are controlled by a sinful self. Apparently for Paul, now that the way of faith has been opened up so that one can live "according to the Spirit," a return to the Law-way is to submit again to the flesh, to a sinful existence. Maybe the Judaizers were preaching that faith is made perfect by works (see Jas. 2:22), suggesting thereby that it takes the works of the law or human, moral works to bring the new life in Christ to perfection. Paul says this is foolishness. The Galatians are not partial Christians, needing a moral supplement. God has done a complete work in their hearts on the condition of their faith in Christ. Having begun *in the spirit* they need only to continue *in the spirit,* that is, to continue to open up their hearts to the Spirit by trust and obedience to Him. He writes later, "If we live by the Spirit, let us also walk (conduct our lives) by the Spirit" (5:25, RSV).

3. *Paul identifies the source of the gift of the Spirit as God himself.* "Does he who supplies the Spirit to you and works miracles among you do so by works of the law, or by the hearing with faith?" (5, RSV). The miracles which are being done among them are evidences of the divine Presence among them. All of this attests that God has and is accepting them as His children. His presence in their

Church's life, in response to their faith, is proof that submission to circumcision and other works of the Law is not required of them either to become or to remain Christians. "So, on every ground, religion based on law cannot explain Christian experience, both at its commencement and during its course."[2]

Abraham, the Father of Faith

Galatians 3:6-9

> 6 Even as Abraham believed God, and it was accounted to him for righteousness.
> 7 Know ye therefore that they which are of faith, the same are the children of Abraham.
> 8 And the scripture, foreseeing that God would justify the heathen through faith, preached before the gospel unto Abraham, saying, In thee shall all nations be blessed.
> 9 So then they which be of faith are blessed with faithful Abraham.

These verses incorporate a second line of attack, not so much upon the Galatians but upon those who are disturbing them. This is a very serious appeal to Scripture, which was accepted as the Word of God by both the Gentile and Jewish Christians. Three aspects of the historical proof are evident in this passage.

1. The Judaizers may have been employing Abraham as their number one example for calling the Galatians to submission to the Law of Moses, especially to the central sign of that fact, namely, circumcision. They may have been saying to the Galatians: "If you Gentiles wish to enjoy all the blessings of righteousness which we enjoy, you must follow the example of our forefather, Abraham, and be circumcised. Then you will be, with us, incorporated into the covenanted people of God." The tragedy of this position is the premise that circumcision was the basic evidence of righteousness for these teachers. Their case rested on Gen. 17:1-14, where it is recorded that God instructed Abraham to seal the covenant between them by submitting to circumcision. But these teachers took the external work of circumcision as of primary importance,

overlooking the more fundamental aspect of Abraham's faith in God.

2. The main thrust of the argument is given in verse 6, which is a direct quotation of the Greek version of Gen. 15:6. It reads: *Even as Abraham believed God, and it was accounted to him for righteousness* (6). One should not think that faith is not part of the Jewish religious tradition. "Faith" for the Jew of Paul's day was trust in and obedience to the Torah, the Law, as bringing righteousness, or acceptance with God. For them, faith was really moral effort, or the attempt to be faithful to the Law. Pauline faith, on the other hand, is a radical surrender to God, who calls sinners through His Word personalized in Jesus Christ.

Faith in no respect can be a moral work of merit. This kind of faith, Paul says, is of the very essence of justification, and it is the kind which our father Abraham had. While his opponents insisted that Abraham was justified by his works, Paul, to the contrary, insisted that he was justified by faith, and he quotes Gen. 15:6 to prove it. This same argument is dealt with at length in Romans 4. There Paul spells out the nature of faith as total self-commitment to Christ, with an acceptance of all that God has done for us in Him, and resulting in justification, and resurrection from the death of sin.

The crux of the argument is stated by Martin as follows: "Abraham was set right with God *before* he practised circumcision, so the Judaizers have given away their case by an appeal to the great founder of O.T. theocracy and the grand exemplar of O.T. piety."[3]

3. The real sons of Abraham are not those who belong to his nation, or those who have practised circumcision as an act of good works, but those who share his faith, and who accept trustingly God's promises. *Know ye therefore that they which are of faith, the same are the children of Abraham* (7). Furthermore, quoting Gen. 12:3, where God pledges that in Abraham *shall all nations be blessed*

(8), Paul asserts that God from the beginning purposed to create a people in Abraham who would become His messengers, proclaiming His love and forgiveness to the whole world. As part of the divine scheme Abraham would be the father of descendants as numerous as the stars in the sky. He believed this promise and God accepted him as the person "to be the foundation stone of his plan for the salvation of the world through Israel."

But Israel, the sons of Abraham, failed in this missionary role. They did not continue to preach this gospel of faith which Abraham had accepted and as a result God reconstituted Israel into the new Israel, the Church, through whom *he would justify the heathen through faith* (8). Men of all races could have come into the historic community of Israel on the basis of their faith in Abraham's God, but that has not happened to any degree until now, Paul writes. The fulfillment of the ancient promise is taking place as people everywhere, including the Galatians, receive by faith the new life in the Spirit. "So then, those who are men of faith are blessed with Abraham who had faith" (9, RSV). Abraham is indeed "the father of us all" (Rom. 4:16).

James Denney spoke of Abraham as the "pattern Christian." And all the New Testament writers who wish to prove anything about true religion say, "Look at Abraham" (see Romans 4; Heb. 6:13-15; 7:1-10; 11:8-19; Jas. 2:21-23).

Deliverance from the Curse of the Law

Galatians 3:10-14

> 10 For as many as are of the works of the law are under the curse: for it is written, Cursed is every one that continueth not in all things which are written in the book of the law to do them.
> 11 But that no man is justified by the law in the sight of God, it is evident: for, The just shall live by faith.
> 12 And the law is not of faith: but, The man that doeth them shall live in them.
> 13 Christ hath redeemed us from the curse of the law, being made a curse for us: for it is written, Cursed is every one that hangeth on a tree.
> 14 That the blessing of Abraham might come on the Gentiles through Jesus Christ; that we might receive the promise of the Spirit through faith.

Paul introduces in this passage a third line of argument as historical proof of his claim of salvation by grace through faith. Scripture not only shows that the true children of Abraham become such by faith and not by the works of the law (more specifically not by circumcision) but the Holy Word also demonstrates that those who rely on the Law for salvation do not receive acceptance with God but rather are placed under a curse. *For as many as are of the works of the law are under the curse: for it is written, Cursed is every one that continueth not in all things which are written in the book of the law to do them* (10). This statement is a paraphrase of Deut. 27:26 which reads: "A curse upon any man who does not fulfil this law by doing all that it prescribes" (NEB).

1. The argument of the Apostle at this point is simple. If the "men of faith" received with Abraham their father the divine blessing, those who are not "men of faith" are "men of the Law," and they are *under the curse*. By *curse*, Paul means the judgment of God. The law-way of salvation promises only failure! Obedient and trustful response to God's call of submission to Him, as characterized the life of Abraham, is the only source of salvation blessing. If one assumes, on the other hand, that keeping a set of rules and thus avoiding transgressions, in one's own strength, is the way of blessing, he is deluded. Salvation blessings do not come by doing but by believing.

Paul further asserts that no person can keep "the whole law." He may have in mind the 613 prescriptions and prohibitions of the Law. The transgression of only one law would imply apostasy and the breaking of the entire covenant relationship with God (see Romans 3; 5:3). The important words in verse 10 are *all things*. "No one could possibly claim that he had fulfilled all the minutiae of Mosaic legislation. Thus he who puts his confidence in his own righteousness, as expressed in law observance, convicts himself of unrighteousness,"[4] writes Blackwood. Winning God's favor by this means leads only to failure and judgment.

2. Pressing on with his argument, Paul says there is only one way to peace with God, that is, the way of faith. *The just shall live by faith* (11). Paul is quoting Hab. 2:4, where the emphasis is more directly upon faithfulness, but there is no essential conflict. Habakkuk says that the righteous man shall live by his faithfulness (see Heb. 10:38). The Apostle here and in Rom. 1:17 stresses justifying faith, which results in faithfulness. The person who is made right with God by faith, and who maintains that relationship, really lives in peace and knows the blessings of God. A devotion to the doing of God's will follows from this justifying relationship to God. This new life is continued and nurtured by the faithful doing of the commands of God (12). Fidelity is one of its essential traits.

3. Since all of us fail miserably and inevitably in this business of "doing" righteousness apart from the dynamic of faith, it becomes necessary for Christ to break *the curse of the law* by *being made a curse for us* (13). He rendered the curse, which the Law imposed on all of us, null and void by taking the curse upon himself, by putting himself in our place, by suffering for us. Thus, the punishment due us would be obviated.

Two things happen when we accept Christ's deed by faith. First, We are incorporated in Him and share His righteousness. We are thus "found in him, not having a righteousness of (our) own, based on law, but that which is through faith in Christ, the righteousness from God that depends on faith" (Phil. 3:9, RSV). Second, the Spirit of Christ provides the wisdom and power to live in accordance with the will of God.

In the Hebrew tradition death upon a cross was considered the most disgraceful fate. Paul quotes from the Old Testament: *Cursed is everyone that hangeth on a tree* (13; Deut. 21:23). Crucifixion was not a Jewish, but a Roman, method of punishment. The usual method of capital punishment practiced by the Jews was stoning. Stephen's case illustrates this fact (Acts 7:57-60). The Law of Moses commanded that Sabbathbreakers, blasphemers, and other lawless persons were to be stoned to death. After the convicted person had been mutilated with rocks, his body was hung from a tree until sundown as a warning to others not to engage in the deed which brought this person to this death. A criminal so executed was thought to have been doomed; indeed he had fallen under the curse of God.

Voluntarily Christ accepted this kind of death for us "lawless ones." However, for us Christians, this Crucified One was not a criminal but the long-awaited Messiah, who suffered for our transgressions and was wounded for our iniquities. The "tree" points to Christ's triumph over every attempt of man to save himself. It declares that faith and faith alone in Him can bring the salvation of God. Martin writes: "The curse which rightfully belongs to a guilty race was voluntarily assumed by One who, although He stood outside it and was therefore blameless, chose to identify Himself with our human misery and need—even to the point of God-forsakenness on the cross."[5]

Christ exhausted the claim of a broken law against those who enter into faith-union with Him. Moreover, the "blessedness" of redemption which Abraham knew as a result of his believing in God is now open to all persons, Jews and Gentiles alike. The new age of God's covenant grace has dawned. The era of Messianic blessedness has arrived with the coming of the Holy Spirit who now indwells the hearts of believers and constitutes the very life of the Church (14).

The Unalterable Covenant

Galatians 3:15-18

> 15 Brethren, I speak after the manner of men; Though it be but a man's covenant, yet if it be confirmed, no man disannulleth, or addeth thereto.
> 16 Now to Abraham and his seed were the promises made. He saith not, And to seeds, as of many; but as of one, And to thy seed, which is Christ.
> 17 And this I say, that the covenant, that was confirmed before of God in Christ, the law, which was four hundred and thirty years after, cannot disannul, that it should make the promise of none effect.

> 18 For if the inheritance be of the law, it is no more of promise: but God gave it to Abraham by promise.

To this point personal experience and Scripture have governed Paul's contest with his Judaizing opponents. Now he turns to reason: *Brethren, I speak after the manner of men* (16). He uses an example from everyday life. The argument proceeds along the following lines:

1. If a man makes a will, only he and nobody else has the right to alter it (15). Clauses cannot be erased from it nor codicils added to it, except by the maker of it. When Abraham heard the call of God, promising him God's blessing upon his life, he responded in faith, and that act of faith was the very essence of the covenant (will) between him and God. That covenant of faith, says Paul, still stands; it has not been altered.

The law which came, indirectly through angels and 430 years after the promise, cannot annul the promise made to Abraham, no more than a person can change the essence of another's will (17). Paul calculates that the actual number of years between Abraham and Moses was 430, apparently following the Greek version of Exod. 12:40. The reference is to the length of time the Israelites were in bondage in Egypt. What Paul has in mind is the long period between the Abrahamic and Mosaic periods in Israel's life. His concern is to show that the revelation of the Law on Mount Sinai in no way cancelled the covenant of faith (will) established by God with Abraham.

2. As a kind of parenthetical thought, the Apostle notes that the promises wrapped up in the covenant were made to Abraham and his seed (16; see Gen. 13:15; 17:7). Apparently Paul's opponents had interpreted "seed" to mean the Jewish people exclusively, based upon the fact that some centuries later than Abraham's time God made a covenant by law with them. Thus, in their judgment the Abrahamic covenant with its promises was superseded by the Mosaic covenant with its law. Paul's answer is negative. He insists that the word "seed" is singular in number

and must be taken as a reference to Christ. But, "seed," though singular, is also collective in meaning, and so conveys the idea that all who turn to Christ in faith are one with Him. So properly, therefore, to be in Christ is tantamount to being a descendant of Abraham or the seed of Abraham.

Christ is a representative figure, incorporating in himself the whole people of God. Paul sees the Church, therefore, as the Body of Christ (see Romans 12; 1 Corinthians 12; Eph. 4:1-16) and at the same time the true children of Abraham. Neil comments that Christ, "the embodiment of the new Israel, the one true Israelite, is the first to receive the promised blessing and becomes the channel through which those who commit themselves to him in faith, whether Jews or Gentiles, likewise share in the benefits which God had from the beginning prepared for his people."[6]

3. The *inheritance* of salvation is essentially the gift of the Spirit (18), as Paul has already suggested in verse 14 and will mention specifically in chapter 5. *Inheritance* refers to the Christian's enjoyment of the Spirit, which is the essence and realization of the ancient promise. Paul uses a strong and important verb in the statement that *God gave it to Abraham by promise* (18). "Has given freely" is a more literal translation. The perfect tense denotes an act begun in the past and continuing into the present. What was initiated by God in His relationship to Abraham is still continuing into the present time in the *seed* of Abraham, Christ. Cole suggests that maybe Paul is thinking of the deeper connotation of grace to the Christian. "For the believer, God's 'grace' is Christ. Paul's use of the perfect tense in this verb is probably deliberate. He wants to stress the 'once-for-allness' of God's grace; no later system of law can alter such a gift to man."[7]

Law and promise are not in opposition. But if the Judaizers insist that the former outmodes or cancels the latter, then "the element of God's grace in *both* dispensations has been denied and the gospel has been subverted (clearly in Rom. 9:6)."[8]

The Real Purpose of the Law

Galatians 3:19-22

> 19 Wherefore then serveth the law? It was added because of transgressions, till the seed should come to whom the promise was made; and it was ordained by angels in the hand of a mediator.
>
> 20 Now a mediator is not a mediator of one, but God is one.
>
> 21 Is the law then against the promises of God? God forbid: for if there had been a law given which could have given life, verily righteousness should have been by the law.
>
> 22 But the scripture hath concluded all under sin, that the promise by faith of Jesus Christ might be given to them that believe.

Paul apparently realizes that those who disagree with his views will raise a question as to the importance of the Law in God's workings in the history of Israel. From all that is said to this point, it would appear that the Law's day is over and mankind is in a new situation. "Why then the law?" (19, RSV). This is the identical question that Paul addresses in Rom. 7:7: "What shall we say then? Is the law sin?" He endeavors to give several reasons for the importance of the Law in the history of salvation.

1. The Law *was added because of transgressions* (19). What this means is problematic. It has been suggested that the Law was added "to restrain fallen human nature." It was a concession on the part of God for the time being because man lacked the moral power to control his sinfulness. The function of the Law was not to make us holy but to make us aware of our sin. The Law served to teach us our moral bankruptcy by making very clear to us what the divine standards require and the penalties for noncompliance. According to the divine plan this task would be brought to an end when *the seed should come to whom the promise was made,* that is, when Christ came.

2. A superior mode of revelation discloses the promise of God and it even takes precedence in the "now" time. The

Law was *ordained by angels in the hand of a mediator* (19b). Moses received the Law indirectly from God by a host of angels (see Deut. 33:2; Acts 7:53; Heb. 2:2 ff) but the promise came to Abraham directly, face-to-face. This contrast is intended to point up the greater importance of the promise. Furthermore, no mediator, even as good as Moses, was needed in the act of revelation to Abraham (20). More specifically, Christ is the embodiment of the promise of grace and He more directly reveals the love and forgiveness of God. "The Word became flesh and dwelt among us, full of grace and truth" (John 1:14, RSV).

3. The human situation under Law attests the failure of the Law to bring men into a right relationship with God, that is, to justify them and to make them righteous. *If there had been a law given which could have given life, verily righteousness should have been by the law. But the scripture hath concluded all under sin* (21-22). The critical issue here is the sinful nature of man. As Martin comments, "The success of the law as an agent of justification is vitiated by human nature which is sinful of itself (Luther's phrase is worth recalling: 'turned in upon itself' and turned away from obedience to God's will) and so impotent."[9] Paul states the issue clearly in Rom. 7:14: "We know that the law is spiritual: but I am carnal, sold under sin." "Law, in these circumstances, is like a railway ticket to a soldier in a prisoner-of-war camp. He *would* use it if he *could*. The help we need must come from outside—from God."[10]

The plight of man attempting to "lift himself by his own bootstraps" is well-known to all of us. The twist in our natures cannot be straightened out by our moral efforts, by all our vain attempts to establish a set of moral dictates and to live by them. Acknowledgment of that fact is the beginning of grace. That is the threshold of hope. Surrender in faith to Christ is the only way to a new and peaceful relationship with God, the actualization of the promised Abrahamic blessing.

The New Order of Faith

Galatians 3:23-29

> 23 But before faith came, we were kept under the law, shut up unto the faith which should afterwards be revealed.
> 24 Wherefore the law was our schoolmaster to bring us unto Christ, that we might be justified by faith.
> 25 But after that faith is come, we are no longer under a schoolmaster.
> 26 For ye are all the children of God by faith in Christ Jesus.
> 27 For as many of you as have been baptized into Christ have put on Christ.
> 28 There is neither Jew or Greek, there is neither bond nor free, there is neither male nor female: for ye are all one in Christ Jesus.
> 29 And if ye be Christ's, then are ye Abraham's seed, and heirs according to the promise.

Paul's picture of man's plight before the coming of Christ is not a pretty one. Society's condition would have been much worse had it not been for the restraining power of law. So, as Neil writes, "Man had to be kept in some kind of order by fear of the consequences of wrongdoing, by a rigid disciplinary code of regulations, by warnings and penalties. But this was not life as life was meant to be."[11] In concluding this chapter, Paul brings together certain concepts which express the assurance of real change in the condition of mankind through faith in Christ Jesus.

1. *The task of the Law as custodian.* Paul puts it this way: *Before faith came, we were kept under the law, shut up unto the faith which should afterwards be revealed. Wherefore the law was our schoolmaster to bring us unto Christ, that we might be justified by faith* (23). "Shut up" really means we were imprisoned and the Law was the jailer. Verse 24 speaks of the Law as *schoolmaster.* The Greek word for schoolmaster is *paidagōgos,* which literally means "child-leader." "Schoolmaster" is hardly the meaning here in Galatians; perhaps something more like "disciplinarian" is needed. Usually, in those days the *paidagōgos* was a faithful slave, entrusted with the care of a child until he reached maturity. His responsibility had to do with the child's moral wellbeing. He was to protect

the child from temptation and danger and to bring him into a wholesome manhood. He accompanied the child wherever he went, to school and to various forms of entertainment. The duties of the *paidagōgos* were more disciplinary than educational.

As applied to the Law, now that Christ has come and the way of faith has been revealed, the custodial, educative work of the Law is completed. Just as the *paidagōgos'* work ended with the child's maturity, so the Law's ministry ended when faith came, when recalcitrant, sinful men entered into the full freedom of life in Christ through faith. A new age dawned, the age of faith.

2. *The children of God.* As Paul says, *Ye are all the children of God by faith in Christ Jesus* (26). Notice the shift from the first person to the second personal plural. From 2:15 to 3:25 Paul has been discussing the situation of the Jewish Christians with whom he belongs racially. Now his attention is turned specifically to the Galatians who are Gentile Christians. The title "children of God" or "sons of God" was normally reserved for Jews and they expected to be given it permanently at the Judgment. The extraordinary thing is that Paul attributes this status to Gentiles now (see Gal. 3:7, 29; 4:6-7, 22, 30; Eph. 1:5).[12] These Gentiles are already (present tense) "sons of God." Paul reminds them that it happened in the past and the status has not changed. The condition for adoption is faith but faith that has an object, Jesus Christ. Faith is not a quality of the human spirit we create in ourselves; rather, it is trustful, obedient, Spirit-inspired response to the Father's call to us in Christ Jesus.

It must be clearly understood that God is Father to us all by virtue of His creation of us (Acts 17:28), but acceptance into His family in a spiritual sense comes only by adoption (see John 1:12).

3. *Initiation into the new family.* Note verse 27: *As many of you as have been baptized into Christ have put on Christ.* Baptism is a public confession of faith and identi-

fication with Christ. *Have put on Christ,* in the original language, really means "have clothed yourselves with Christ." Barclay notes that, in the ancient Church "the candidate for baptism was clothed in pure white robes, symbolic of the new life into which he had entered. Just as the initiate put on his new white robe he put on Christ; his life was clothed with Christ."[13]

This act of grace was a public testimony that one "shared a common parentage—with a family likeness."

4. *A new unity of fellowship.* Paul affirms: *There is neither Jew nor Greek, there is neither bond nor free, there is neither male nor female; for ye are all one in Christ Jesus* (28). The Jew-Gentile issue lay in the background of this struggle with the Judaizers. The unhealthy, disruptive pride of position and heritage on the part of these Jewish opponents was about to destroy the youthful Church. But Paul was determined that would not happen. There must be an unbroken fellowship in Christ Jesus. A son of God is a son of God! There are no second-class citizens in the Church of Jesus Christ! Racial prejudice, social division, sexual inequality are intolerable in the community of believers. (see Eph. 2:11-22). When we are baptized into Christ, we become one people!

5. *The sons of Abraham.* Verse 29 reads: *If ye be Christ's, then are ye Abraham's seed, and heirs according to the promise.* This summarizing statement reaches well back into the argument, particularly to 3:16. Christ is the *seed* of Abraham, the Mediator of this way of faith, and all who are in Him share in the faith-family of Abraham. Also, the Galatians are *heirs according to the promise,* meaning that the promise of Abraham has also come to fulfillment in them because they are "in Christ."

Faith-union with Christ brings us into the True Israel. We therefore receive the benefits which God decreed long ago should come to the descendants of Abraham. All peoples have this privilege of identification opened to them because the way of faith has been inaugurated through Christ. Faith is a free act of the whole being. It has no preconditions of moral effort or of religious heritage. Every person, therefore, Jew or Greek, can come to Christ, trusting only in His shed blood, and be saved. No longer need anyone struggle with the Law, striving to save himself. He can receive by faith the recreating, cleansing, empowering Spirit who will channel the works of Christ through his life as he continues to live in faith.

GALATIANS 4

What Heirship Means

Galatians 4:1-7

> 1 Now I say, That the heir, as long as he is a child, differeth nothing from a servant, though he be lord of all;
> 2 But is under tutors and governors until the time appointed of the father.
> 3 Even so we, when we were children, were in bondage under the elements of the world:
> 4 But when the fulness of the time was come, God sent forth his Son, made of a woman, made under the law,
> 5 To redeem them that were under the law, that we might receive the adoption of sons.
> 6 And because ye are sons, God hath sent forth the Spirit of his Son into your hearts, crying, Abba, Father.
> 7 Wherefore thou art no more a servant, but a son; and if a son, then an heir of God through Christ.

A shift in the argument takes place with the opening of chapter 4. The previous section set forth the major point that, with the coming of Christ, God's promise to Abraham was realized. Christ is "the true seed" of Abraham. And by using the word "seed" both as a singular and collective noun, Paul asserts that all who are baptized into Christ are one with Him and with Abraham. So Christ is "the corporate Christ" and the Church, the company of believers, is His Body, sharing His life and mission in the world.

The specific link with chapter 3 is found in the idea of

a child under the leadership of the *paidagōgos,* the schoolmaster (3:24).

1. *Slavery and sonship* (1-3). A young child (the Greek word used here can mean "babe," but probably should carry the idea of a "minor"), as long as he has not arrived at legal maturity, lives pretty much as one of the servants or slaves in his father's house. He may be *the heir* of all that his father owns, and if so, he is the *lord of all.* But his present existence as a child is very much like that of a slave. He is subordinated to *tutors and governors* (2), or better "guardians" and "trustees" (RSV). In this instance *paidagōgos* may refer to the Law, but we cannot be certain. The point to be made, however, is that before one's conversion the will of other persons controlled his life. The "keepers of the Law" imposed the works-way of salvation upon him, or he thought he could develop an acceptable moral life-style on his own which would make him the inheritor of the blessings of God. The result of all this effort was only the continuance of spiritual slavery.

Our enslavement, apart from Christ, was one of being *under the elements of the world* (3). Other versions of the Bible translate *world* as "universe" (RSV, NEB). The *elements* has been variously interpreted by scholars. Some take it to mean "elementary principles" or "alphabet," the reference being to "elementary stages of religious experience (whether Jewish or Gentile) through which they have gone in the past, but which are now out-dated by Christ."[14] The Galatians were Gentiles and it would not be proper to say that they were under the domination of the Jewish Law. But they were living under the power of ineffectual and unsatisfying religious views—*weak and beggarly elements* (9). These "elements" were comparatively worthless.

Other commentators have concluded that the phrase "the elements of the world" refers to astrological beliefs. The reference in verse 10 to *days, and months, and times, and years,* along with Col. 2:8, suggests a primitive association of spiritual forces with the earth, air, fire, water (the elements), and the stars. Maybe some of the Jews in the region where the Galatian Christians lived had embraced this kind of philosophy. If the missionaries Paul was opposing were "pure Jews" this interpretation will hardly stand, for they would have resisted such blending of their faith with contemporary pagan ideas.

The Galatians as Gentile pagans would, however, understand Paul's thought on this matter. Before their conversion, in their struggles to find peace in the midst of their threatening world, they quickly embraced such farfetched concepts. They were not unlike many people today, who turn quickly to the esoteric teachings of Eastern gurus or to the astrologers, to find some hope for their restless hearts, but to no avail. Christ dwelling within is the only way of peace. He is the Prince of Peace.

Paul had no doubts about the demonic powers at work in the universe, and he knew the evil forces would use every possible means to distort the truth and to bring the hearts of men into captivity. He wrote to the Ephesians: "We are not contending against flesh and blood, but against the principalities, against the powers, against the world rulers of this present darkness, against the spiritual hosts of wickedness in the heavenly places" (6:12, RSV).

Finally, the Apostle is saying that all human religions, Jewish and Gentile alike, eventually lead men into spiritual bondage. Men who embrace them live in mortal fear of doing something offensive to the alleged deities and thus face punishment. They are helpless victims before arbitrary powers. The choices offered both Jews and Gentiles, before the coming of Christ, left much to be desired. Slavery rather than sonship characterized the life of men until Christ's advent.

2. *The Slave who became the Liberator* (4). "With the Incarnation the whole human situation was transformed. The day of man's servitude was past."[15] *When the fulness of the time was come, God sent forth his Son, made of a*

woman, made under the law (4). Four noteworthy truths are wrapped up in this pivotal verse.

a. The fulness of the time. Obviously, the reference goes back to verse 2: "Until the date set by the father" (RSV). The father of a minor determines when he will release his will for the benefit of the child. God had a time, set according to His clock of redemption, when He would invade man's earthly existence through the enfleshment of His Son, Christ Jesus. This was the moment when all God's preparations for His grand thrust of salvation were complete. All that had gone on in previous centuries by way of teaching and directing called for this decisive action.

Now His covenant will, with all its saving benefits, was revealed to mankind. It was God's time, not the hour demanded by mankind. He determined it; the love beat of His heart said the saving moment had come. The prophetic word of the preachers of old came into fulfillment and all the blessings of the Mosaic order were now superceded by the blessings of the Christ order.

b. God sent forth His Son. Two interesting thoughts are expressed in this sentence.

First, the Son is sent from the Father; He is among us to do a task for the Father. The verbal form "sent" is the one from which we get "apostle," which means "sent one" or "messenger." Jesus himself said, "I must work the works of him who sent me" (John 9:4). He is the Great Apostle who not only proclaims the Word of God but is also in himself, the Word of God. He said to His disciples: "As the Father has sent me, even so I send you" (John 20:21, RSV). When we take up that responsibility, we become with Him apostles of the Father.

Second, Paul sees Jesus as more than the Messiah of the Jews, which He indeed was. He is primarily the Son of God, begotten of the Father before the foundation of the world. The Son is not a person adopted by God from among men. Rather, He is one with the Father and shares all the powers of the Father. Therefore, His coming is a unique act, in that the God of the universe takes on the nature of man.

c. Made of a woman. Literally, in the original language this phrase expresses the idea of the birth of a human being "out of" a human mother. The reference here is not primarily to the Virgin Birth, though that is implied by the specific reference to woman and not to man. Rather, it is intended to declare His full humanity. Neil comments that the phrase means that He "entered into our human situation as one of ourselves."[16] Christ became like us in order that we might become like Him. He experienced all the sinful threats common to our existence, for God sent Him "in the likeness of sinful flesh and for sin" that He might condemn "sin in the flesh" (Rom. 8:3, RSV). "Flesh" in this instance means humanity. We can take heart, therefore, as we come to Christ, for we know He can sympathize with us as we struggle with sin (see Heb. 2:17-18; 4:14-16).

d. Made under the law. Christ came "not only as a man of a particular race, at a particular time and in a particular place, but as one who shared the frustration of being subjected to the domination of the very system from which He came to deliver us. He became a slave so that we might be free."[17] Adam Clarke comments that Christ came into subjection to the law that "all its designs might be fulfilled, and by his *death* the whole might be abolished; the *law* dying when the Son of God expired upon the cross."[18] It would seem that when Paul omits the article before *law,* he may have had more in mind than the Jewish Law. He understood that all men were under some form of law. If so, then the intent is to emphasize again that the old order of seeking acceptance with God by good works, however nobly prompted, has been set aside, and every man's hope lies in a personal relationship to Christ.

3. *The redemption Christ brings* (5-7). These verses

majestically express the purpose of the sending of the Son into our blighted order and lives. *Redeem* in this verse means literally to "buy" or "buy up" and it carries all the implications of a person purchasing the rights of freedom of citizenship for a slave. Gal. 3:13 speaks of being "redeemed . . . from the curse of the law," but here the redemption is even greater; it is freedom from the law itself, that is, from the law "as a system of attempted self-justification." The benefits of that glorious act are three.

a. The adoption as sons (5). The word "adoption" is found only here and in four other places in the New Testament (Rom. 8:15, 23; 9:4; Eph. 1:5). Sonship is not exclusively a Pauline idea; John speaks of it also in 1 John 3:2. The important note for Paul is that the enjoyment of that relationship comes through adoption. The concept is rooted in the Old Testament where it refers to God's choice of Israel from among all the nations to be His child. Though sons by creation, we became orphans by our sin, but we have been taken back into the family of God. Moreover, that adoption as sons means we are also sons of Abraham.

A new relationship in the family of God takes place when, by faith, we are joined to Christ. While status as sons is indeed included in this concept, as Neil says, "What Christ has done is not to make a book entry in a divine ledger, which balances up what we have failed to do with what he has done on our behalf. Paul now shows that the result of what Christ has done is essentially not to give us a new *status* but a new attitude to God."[19]

b. The witness of the Spirit in our hearts. Here is proof that one is a son of God. *God hath sent forth the Spirit of his Son into your hearts, crying, Abba, Father* (6, see Rom. 8:14-17). On his own the sinner cannot really say "Father" to God, but the believer in his heart can say "Father" because the Spirit of Christ within him enables him to do so. Howard comments, "This is the filial cry, from a loving son, upon the recognition of a loving Father."[20]

One of the strong and renewed notes in the revival under John and Charles Wesley was that of the witness of the Holy Spirit to the believer's heart that he truly belongs to God. Indeed, the Wesleys insisted that this witness was an essential part of both the saving and sanctifying experiences. "Salvation is by faith, but such faith has its response. It is wondrously and gloriously personal, God suiting to each soul the manifestation of himself that results in the cry—*Abba, Father*."[21] The assurance of adoption does not fail to come to our hearts when we unreservedly respond to God's call to repent and believe in Christ, or when we consecrate ourselves to God and trust Him for cleansing.

c. *The confirmation of inheritance* (7). We are no longer servants but sons, and thence, heirs of God. Here is the completion of the idea expressed in verses 1-3. The slave is governed, subservient, and bound, but the son is free, having been redeemed from the bondage of pursuing the way of law and is now living by faith. All the blessings promised to Abraham, God's original heir, accrue to the believer. Christ himself shares in those blessings, being the Seed of Abraham, but He also mediates the grace which makes them available to all who follow Him in faith.

Falling into Slavery

Galatians 4:8-11

> 8 Howbeit then, when ye knew not God, ye did service unto them which by nature are no gods.
> 9 But now, after that ye have known God, or rather are known of God, how turn ye again to the weak and beggarly elements, whereunto ye desire again to be in bondage?
> 10 Ye observe days, and months, and times, and years.
> 11 I am afraid of you, lest I have bestowed upon you labour in vain.

Paul is utterly amazed that these Galatians would ever want to return to the life which they once knew. They lived under a constant fear of the man-made gods and the unpredictable natural forces. He writes: "Formerly, when you did not acknowledge God, you were the slaves of beings which in their nature are no gods," or as the footnote has it, "were slaves to 'gods' which in reality do not exist" (8, NEB). The reference is to the polytheism of paganism which controlled their pre-Christian lives. The Apostle is also aware of their spiritual ignorance; they did not have the privilege of living in the Hebrew tradition in which the truth of the one true and living God was faithfully preached and believed. Now that they have come into this new "knowledge," why would they want to fall back into fear and despair?

Three penetrating spiritual insights as to the nature of Christian freedom surface at this point in Paul's dispute with the Galatians.

1. *The Christian experience of God is "the knowledge of God."* Paul asks, *Now, after that ye have known God, or rather are known of God, how turn ye again to the weak and beggarly elements whereunto ye desire again to be in bondage?* (9). Their faith in Christ had brought them into relationship with God and it was their *believing* that brought about this *knowing.* John writes: "No one has ever seen God: the only Son, who is in the bosom of the Father, he has made him known" (1:18, RSV). Jesus says: "All things have been delivered to me by my Father; and no one knows the Son except the Father, and no one knows the Father except the Son and any one to whom the Son chooses to reveal him" (Matt. 11:27, RSV).

Knowledge here is not the knowledge of intellectual assent but rather the knowledge of acquaintance, of intimacy, of person-to-person relationship. "To know God" is "to love and obey God, to submit to His lordship over one's life." For the Galatians, and for us, too, this knowledge comes only when there is a decisive break with the old idolatrous, fearful, self-centered existence.

Paul qualified his statement by saying that his readers *are known of God* (9). He wants always to give God the glory for any Christian experience. As Ridderbos explains,

"The bond uniting them with God was not established by them but by God himself. He had wanted to know them as His own, interested Himself in their behalf, had chosen them. There lay the secret of the change."[22] To "know" God, or "to be known" by God is to be accepted by Him, to be changed, to be adopted into His family, and to be an heir with Christ.

2. *Turning back to the old life is a retreat to spiritual weakness and poverty* (9). The "elementary things" are *weak* because they only enhance the fear and guilt of sin in our lives. It is true about the law-way of living as well as the vain religious commitments of paganism. There is no forgiveness of sin; there is only the continual struggle to appease "the god who does not live" and therefore is unable to help.

Moreover, the "elementary things" are poverty-stricken because they lack the riches of grace. They have nothing to give the sinner, they only rob the soul of hope and peace. The person living under their dominion never can know the peace and sufficiency of the divine life in his soul. Apart from faith, he wrestles despairingly with every sinful act, trying to find inner relief and release, but these blessings never come because *the weak and beggarly elements* cannot give them. In Christ, to the contrary, there is complete and lasting satisfaction and resourcefulness for the whole of one's existence, because God who is rich in love and mercy has accepted him as His child.

3. *For the Christian, every day is God's day.*[23] This is the reverse truth of verse 10: *Ye observe days, and months, and times, and years.* It may well be that these Galatians were so immersed in the Jewish Law by this time they were observing all the Jewish special days and seasons. The Law provided a lengthy calendar of religious days which the faithful Jew was expected to keep in reverence.

Barclay sees the reference to these special festivals and fasts as suggesting our tendency to divide the calendar into sacred and secular days, days which belong to

God and days which belong to man and in which he can do as he pleases. Such a division presents the temptation to think that one has discharged his religious duties when he has properly observed the special days. The truth is that "for the Christian every day is God's day." To live each day for God calls for a large measure of His wisdom and grace. Given this threat to the spiritual lives of the Galatians, it is no wonder that Paul's shepherd heart cries out, "You make me fear that all the pains I spent on you may prove to be labour lost" (11, NEB).

An Appeal from the Heart

Galatians 4:12-20

> 12 Brethren, I beseech you, be as I am; for I am as ye are: ye have not injured me at all.
> 13 Ye know how through infirmity of the flesh I preached the gospel unto you at the first.
> 14 And my temptation which was in my flesh ye despised not, nor rejected; but received me as an angel of God, even as Christ Jesus.
> 15 Where is then the blessedness ye spake of? for I bear you record, that, if it had been possible, ye would have plucked out your own eyes, and have given them to me.
> 16 Am I therefore become your enemy, because I tell you the truth?
> 17 They zealously affect you, but not well; yea, they would exclude you, that ye might affect them.
> 18 But it is good to be zealously affected always in a good thing, and not only when I am present with you.
> 19 My little children, of whom I travail in birth again until Christ be formed in you,
> 20 I desire to be present with you now, and to change my voice; for I stand in doubt of you.

Paul interrupts his appeal to reason and Scripture to make an appeal from his heart: *Brethren, I beseech you* (12). This is not a strange turn, for Paul knows that "every theological argument implies the heart and the will as well as the intellect."[24] The essence of the appeal is that the Galatians *be as I am,* by which he means that, since he severed his relationships with the old legalism and with his inherited religion when he accepted Christ and became an ambassador to the Gentiles, they should do likewise. He begs them to adopt the same attitude toward the now-outdated Jewish law that now characterized his life. In effect, he says, "Meet me on my grounds now just as I met you on your grounds when I first came to you."

Attitudes sometimes become barriers to communications. Paul perceives this to be the situation with the Galatians. So, he endeavors to open their hearts by reminding them of his ministry among them, a ministry in which he preached faithfully that faith, and not religious works, is the one condition for acceptance with God. Even though he discerns that a change in their attitude had taken place, he writes, *Ye have not injured me at all.*

1. Paul recalls the reception they gave him at the beginning of his ministry (13-15). He arrived in Galatia with an *infirmity of the flesh* (13). He was a sick man. Was he plagued with that which he refers to in 2 Cor. 12:7 as "a thorn in the flesh"? Though Paul was a man of faith and true piety, he was not exempt from illness. Many good Christians suffer from serious ailments, but no preaching, such as we sometimes hear from alleged faith-healers, should be allowed to impose guilt upon them. Sickness is not sin. False guilt adds psychological pain to the physical pain they already endure.

Various theories have been advanced as to the nature of the "thorn." It could be persecution, physical appearance (see 2 Cor. 10:10), eye disease *(If it had been possible, ye would have plucked out your own eyes, and have given them to me* [15]), or malaria and the consequent severe headaches produced by it. Acts 13:13-14 records that when Paul, Barnabas, and Mark came to Perga in Pamphylia, they did not linger in the lowlands there, which were notorious for their epidemics of malaria. Mark left them there but they moved on northward to the highlands near Antioch in Pisidia. This old theory hypothesizes that Paul contracted malaria in the lowlands and therefore fled to the plains around Antioch for relief. Thus, he arrived among the Galatians a sick man, suffering from prostrating headaches. We cannot say for certain that Paul is referring to this type of sickness.

At any rate, there may have been something about his appearance which was unsightly, but the Galatians did not reject him because of it. A better translation of verse 14 is: "Though my condition was a trial to you, you did not scorn or despise me, but received me as an angel of God, as Christ Jesus" (RSV). The reception was overwhelming; they considered him a messenger of God, even Christ himself.

Paul is amazed at the transformation which has taken place in them. So he asks, *Where is then the blessedness ye spake of?* (15) or, "What has become of the satisfaction you felt?" (RSV). Where is all the happiness we enjoyed together? Paul inquires. The Galatians would have done anything humanly possible at that time, even to the plucking out of their eyes, to help this grand missionary. Now he felt himself to be their enemy (16).

2. *Paul is repulsed by the deceitful intentions of his Judaizing opponents* and by the effect of their teachings on the Galatians (17-20). "They make much of you, but for no good purpose; they want to shut you out, that you may make much of them" (17, RSV). These false teachers apparently wanted to keep the Galatians away from Paul, and consequently shut away from liberty in Christ. As Martin remarks, they "quenched the Galatians 'conquering newborn joy' in Christ (15) and arrested their growth in Christlikeness" (19).[25] By the time of his writing they should have become full-grown men and women in Christ.

Paul's agonizing concern is expressed in the unique illustration of a woman in birth pangs—*of whom I travail in birth again until Christ be formed in you* (19). It may be that Paul is thinking of the embryo developing in the womb. So when we believe on the Lord Jesus, He comes into our hearts to form His life in us. Stagg writes, "Salvation is not a matter of ritual performance, creedal confession, or hitch-hiking on divine transactions. . . . Salvation means nothing less than Christ's penetration of our deepest inner self to transform it. . . . He [Paul] will suffer 'birth pangs' for them until they 'become pregnant with Christ'!"[26] The key word in this verse is the word *again*. It may mean that Paul is thinking that real apostasy has taken place among the Galatians and now birth pangs must be experienced by him again as he attempts to bring them back to Christ.

Perhaps Paul is suggesting the pain which a mother endures whenever her child does wrong. The Apostle is agonizing over the potential or real spiritual failure of the Galatians because they listen to the false teachers.

The cry of his aching, yet love-filled heart is expressed in the familiar address: *My little children* (see 1 Cor. 4:14; 2 Cor. 6:13). Writing a letter is the best he can do now, but his deepest desire is to see them face-to-face. He is very baffled by their behavior. *I stand in doubt of you*, he writes or, "I am at my wits' end about you" (20, NEB). Cole reminds us that it is "false to think of Paul merely as the prince of evangelists; he was also the prince of pastors."[27]

An Old Testament Lesson

Galatians 4:21-31

21 Tell me, ye that desire to be under the law, do ye not hear the law?
22 For it is written, that Abraham had two sons, the one by a bondmaid, the other by a freewoman.
23 But he who was of the bondwoman was born after the flesh; but he of the freewoman was by promise.
24 Which things are an allegory: for these are the two covenants; the one from the mount Sinai, which gendereth to bondage, which is Agar.
25 For this Agar is mount Sinai in Arabia, and answereth to Jerusalem which now is, and is in bondage with her children.
26 But Jerusalem which is above is free, which is the mother of us all.
27 For it is written, Rejoice, thou barren that bearest not; break forth and cry, thou that travailest not: for the desolate hath many more children than she which hath an husband.
28 Now we, brethren, as Isaac was, are the children of promise.
29 But as then he that was born after the flesh persecuted him that was born after the Spirit, even so it is now.
30 Nevertheless what saith the scripture? Cast out the bondwoman and her son: for the son of the bondwoman shall not be heir with the son of the freewoman.
31 So then, brethren, we are not children of the bondwoman, but of the free.

After the interlude with its personal appeal, Paul returns to his argumentative form. The style of debate is typical of the rabbis, the great teachers of Paul's day and under whom he studied in Jerusalem. Perhaps the Galatians had become acquainted with this type of argument through listening to the Judaizers, who insisted on their coming under the Mosaic Law if they hoped to be genuine Christians. Paul shows himself to be a bit testy at this point. In effect, he writes, "If you insist on using the old rabbinic method of interpretation, let's hear what the Scripture has to say, first, and then interpret it" (21). So, Paul turns to a very familiar story from the life of their spiritual father, Abraham (Genesis 16, 21).

1. *The two covenants*—the covenant of works and the covenant of grace—are illustrated in the lives of Hagar and Sarah, the two wives of Abraham. The contrast between the two can best be seen in parallel columns:

Hagar, the slave	Sarah, the free woman
Ishmael, the child of flesh	Isaac, the child of promise
The earthly Jerusalem	The heavenly Jerusalem
Bondage	Freedom
Sterility	Fruitfulness
Salvation by law	Salvation by grace
The old covenant	The new covenant

The intention of this allegory—a story in which the meaning is brought from the outside and is not inherent in the obvious elements in it—is to show that the Jews, who rejected Jesus, are really descendants of Ishmael, the child of slavery, and therefore are themselves slaves. Christians are descendants of Isaac, the child of promise and freedom, and are themselves free persons. The new covenant bypasses the covenant of Sinai because it has been fulfilled in Christ. Hagar's lineage leads to the earthly Jerusalem and all that it stands for by way of works-righteousness, but Sarah's lineage brings one into the heavenly Jerusalem, the true home of Christ's people (see Heb. 12:22; Rev. 3:12; 21:2).

"The heavenly Jerusalem" is now a present reality in the Church and is to be identified with the kingdom of God. It was inaugurated by Christ and proclaimed by the Church, but is not synonymous with it. The Church is "a colony of the Kingdom": it is not the Kingdom in the totality of its life and power, though it shares in its life. The powers of the Heavenly Order are being felt in the Church and all Christians have a foretaste of the glory of the Heavenly Order which will burst upon the world in God's time. We have "a little bit of heaven to go to heaven in" (to quote a familiar spiritual adage).

2. Paradoxically, Sarah, the "birthless" woman becomes the mother of many children. Paul quotes from Isa. 54:1: *Rejoice, thou barren that bearest not; break forth and cry, thou that travailest not: for the desolate hath many more children than she which hath an husband* (27). Obviously, Paul is playing on Sarah's loss of hope of having a child while Hagar, the slave woman, had given her husband Ishmael. Now, however, amazingly, she has more children than Hagar. While the argument is a bit complex, the point Paul is making is clear. By faith in Christ we have become children of God's promise, like Isaac (28). We are thus Sarah's children and not Hagar's. Sarah's true children are those who have faith in God for their salvation, whatever their ethnic or cultic background. And there are countless numbers of them! *So then, brethren, we are not children of the bondwoman, but of the free* (31).

3. Legalism must be driven out of the churches of Galatia (29-30). Just as Isaac was persecuted by Ishmael (see Gen. 21:9), so today the children of promise are being persecuted by the children of bondage. The two lines of salvation—by works and by faith—are irreconcilable. The two cannot co-exist in the same spiritual family because they are diametrically opposed to one another. This is the reason for the persecution. Stagg states this truth emphatically:

God's children born of God's Spirit are persecuted by the legalist whose highest allegiance is to the Law. Just see who has persecuted whom throughout Christian history! In the world, legally free people have persecuted slaves. In religion, persecution comes usually by slaves to some creedal stereotype, ceremonial rite, or code of culture. Jesus is crucified, Stephen is stoned, and Tyndale is burned at the stake—by what kind of religious people? They are legalists all![28]

Moreover, all this strongly hints that Paul is wanting the Galatians to drive out all Judaizing influences among them (30). Just as Sarah, the free woman, drove out Hagar, the slave woman with her son, because they could not share the same house, so the Galatians must cast out those who are trying to lead them into spiritual slavery again. Let it be clearly understood that Paul believes that "Jew and Gentile may and will co-exist in the Christian Church—but only as 'Isaac,' not as 'Ishmael.' Unbelieving Israel is excluded from blessing."[29]

Christianity is the good news of the liberation of the human heart, through the Spirit of Christ, from all the forces that seek to enslave it. Thus, any interpretation of the Christian faith that tries to bind it to rules and regulations, as if these can bring salvation, must be steadfastly resisted. True freedom comes through trustful and obedient response to the loving Father. This is the bedrock truth about salvation.

It has been said that "the New Testament does not say, 'You shall know the rules, and by them you shall be bound,' but 'You shall know the truth, and the truth shall make you free.'" What is the truth that makes free? God in Christ Jesus justifies, acquits, makes righteous, and keeps in right relationship with himself all who believe and continue to believe in Him as the loving, forgiving Father.

The Life of Freedom

Galatians 5:1-26

GALATIANS 5

The Tragedy of Turning Back

Galatians 5:1-5

> 1 Stand fast therefore in the liberty wherewith Christ hath made us free, and be not entangled again with the yoke of bondage.
> 2 Behold, I Paul say unto you, that if ye be circumcised, Christ shall profit you nothing.
> 3 For I testify again to every man that is circumcised, that he is a debtor to do the whole law.
> 4 Christ is become of no effect unto you, whosoever of you are justified by the law; ye are fallen from grace.
> 5 For we through the Spirit wait for the hope of righteousness by faith.

Paul has argued from *history* in chapters 1 and 2, from *theology* in chapters 3 and 4, and now in chapters 5 and 6 he employs the *moral* argument. All of these arguments intertwine and the final effect is overpowering. In these final two sections the Apostle rises to the peak of his inspiration as he further elucidates what freedom really means for the believer. In chapter 5, Paul concerns himself with two issues essentially: The need to utterly reject legalism because of the serious consequences of a failure to do so, and the need to understand what freedom means in daily living. Stagg writes: "He holds freedom in Christ to be non-negotiable, and he holds that freedom must be exercised responsibly. The outcome is to be in terms of the 'fruit of the Spirit' and not 'the works of the flesh.'"[1]

Verse 1 of chapter 5 both summarizes what Paul has been declaring to this point and projects a fresh emphasis on freedom. It also incorporates a command. "It is for freedom that Christ has set us free. Stand firm, then, and do not let yourselves be burdened again by a yoke of slavery" (NIV). Christian freedom is costly. We enjoy it, but all too often we surrender it by slipping back into religious ways of behavior which are simply "works of righteousness." Faith no longer guides and inspires our living. We simply go through the rituals and conform to the rules as if that is the heart of it all. We have a "form of godliness" but have not the power of a living Christ within (see 2 Tim. 3:5). A lifetime responsibility falls upon the Christian to preserve his freedom by constant faith in Christ. Betz comments with insight: "Freedom is not merely a theory but an experience of freedom."[2] Faith in Christ creates that experience and faith maintains it.

Paul lays down a challenge to the Galatians to face up to the implications of their tendency to listen to the Judaizers. What is happening to them is not a minor matter. They cannot casually introduce some Jewish elements into their Christian lives and think it makes no difference. Likewise, we cannot happily incorporate elements of other religions and the culture in which we live and think we can maintain the freedom which faith in Christ has brought us. Christ must be central and singular in our lives.

1. Paul makes clear to the Galatians that it is Christ, not circumcision, which identifies them as God's people. *I Paul say unto you, that if ye be circumcised, Christ shall profit you nothing* (2). The agitators in Galatia were insisting that circumcision was the absolutely necessary evidence of acceptance with God. True children of Abraham, they said, are those who bear in their bodies that specific mark of identification. Paul would agree that it might be acceptable for the Jew, but not for the Gentile. It was irrelevant to their faith. Neil's comments on circumcision are very sane:

> It was an ancient practice, hallowed by centuries of loyal observance, meaningful in a particular his-

torical setting in that it bound together the sons of Israel as the special channel of God's revelation before the coming of Christ. Since the coming of Christ, loyalty to race, tradition and religious heritage made circumcision still a proper practice for Christians of Jewish extraction. But it must be no more than that. Neither must it be treated as a religious fetish nor must this external act, however rich in meaning, be equated in importance with the act of allegiance, involving the whole personality, whereby a man handed over his life to God as he had come to know him in Jesus Christ.[3]

Later on in the chapter, the Apostle states frankly that *in Jesus Christ neither circumcision availeth any thing, nor uncircumcision* (6). Faith is the reality of the Christian life, not any external sign or ceremonial practice. Long ago, the prophet Samuel enunciated this basic truth: "Behold, to obey is better than sacrifice" (1 Sam. 15:22). Quite obviously he was talking about the obedience of faith.

2. Paul lists four results which will inevitably follow if the law-way of righteousness is reintroduced.

a. Christ shall profit you nothing (2), or, "Christ will be of no advantage to you" (RSV). Accepting circumcision is tantamount to accepting the Law as the hope of acceptance with God. That would cancel out the benefits of the work of Christ in their hearts.

b. You are *a debtor to do the whole law* (3). This means that one has committed himself once again to an impossible standard. Paul has already argued this issue (3:10; see 6:13). There is no possibilitiy of sinners ever accumulating enough merit by good deeds to gain entrance into the kingdom of God. Martin says it succinctly: "We have shut and bolted the door to God's Kingdom *on our side.*"[4]

c. Christ is become of no effect unto you (4). The meaning here is much stronger than the KJV indicates. Paul really is saying that they are "alienated from Christ"

(NIV), or "severed from Christ" (RSV). The Greek verb in this reference has the meaning of "being cut off from relations with someone or something" (see Rom. 7:2, 6). We are talking here about two exclusive principles—Christ, and the Law (represented by circumcision). To accept one is to reject the other. "You must have the law and no Christ, or Christ and no law, for your *justification.*"[5] The Jew who accepts Christ may continue in his Jewish practices, but by virtue of his coming to Christ, he has demonstrated the need of Christ. But for a Gentile to turn to the Law as a necessary aspect of his salvation is to declare that Christ and grace are not enough for him. "By implication, then 'Christ' is no longer a savior and 'grace' is no longer grace. As a result, such people do not merely change 'denominations,' but become real converts to non-Christian Judaism."[6] At that point the relationship with Christ, which brings inward peace and freedom, is broken and one is back in the old life.

d. You are *fallen from grace* (4). This note touches the heart of Paul's warning. "Grace" is the unmerited favor of God toward repentant sinners. It describes the gift of forgiveness and newness of life freely offered by God through Jesus Christ. It has been said that "grace is God in action for the salvation of sinful men." That divine action is uniquely expressed in the death and resurrection of His Son. Grace, therefore, includes Christ because He is the supreme expression and meaning of grace. "The Word became flesh and dwelt among us, full of grace and truth" (John 1:14, RSV). To reject Christ therefore is to *fall from grace,* or, to fall out of the domain of His favor. In Rom. 5:1-2, Paul writes: "Since we are justified by faith, we have peace with God through our Lord Jesus Christ. Through him we have obtained access to this grace in which we stand, and we rejoice in our hope of sharing the glory of God" (RSV).

In contrast to the Galatians, Paul, along with those who agree with him, *through the Spirit wait for the hope of righteousness by faith* (5). Righteousness is not the content of hope because it is already possessed by faith, explains Howard. The hope which righteousness inspires includes the assurance that trust in Christ will result finally in full and complete acceptance with God.

Love, the Essence of the Free Life

Galatians 5:6-12

> 6 For in Jesus Christ neither circumcision availeth any thing, nor uncircumcision; but faith which worketh by love.
> 7 Ye did run well; who did hinder you that ye should not obey the truth?
> 8 This persuasion cometh not of him that calleth you.
> 9 A little leaven leaveneth the whole lump.
> 10 I have confidence in you through the Lord, that ye will be none otherwise minded: but he that troubleth you shall bear his judgment, whosoever he be.
> 11 And I, brethren, if I yet preach circumcision, why do I yet suffer persecution? then is the offence of the cross ceased.
> 12 I would they were even cut off which trouble you.

1. One of Paul's most magnificent expressions appears in verse 6: *faith which worketh by love*. It has been translated in several captivating ways: "faith working through love" (RSV); "faith active in love" (NEB); "faith expressing itself through love" (NIV). Faith is the plant of the Christian life and love is its bloom, its flower. Using our Lord's beautiful analogy of the vine and the branches, faith grafts us into the vine, Christ Jesus, and love is the fruit of that union. "I am the vine, ye are the branches: He that abideth in me, and I in him, the same bringeth forth much fruit: for without me ye can do nothing" (John 15:5).

Jesus and Paul converge in their teaching quite precisely here. No man can expect to produce the fruit of holiness except as he abides in Christ, for it is Christ who supplies the pure life-flow which forms and nourishes the deeds acceptable to God. We are "created in Christ Jesus unto good works" (Eph. 2:10).

> "Faith working through love", therefore, means "a faith that performs good works through love," according to Luther. "Idle faith," he writes, "is not justifying faith. . . . Inwardly it consists in faith toward God, outwardly in love toward our fellow-man."[7]

2. An interlude is introduced at this point which shows us a bit of impatience on the part of Paul (7-12). We should not be too hard on him, however. The impatience is generated out of his genuine love for his converts. He questions them: *Ye did run well; who did hinder you* ["cut in on you," NIV] *that ye should not obey the truth?* (7). Paul knew the answer to this rhetorical query, but he records it to be certain that the Galatians understand his concern. This new *persuasion* to place one's confidence in circumcision and the Law did not derive from God who called them. He indeed would be no party to this denial of the primacy of faith. The Judaizers were the culprits. To further emphasize his point, Paul quotes an old maxim: *A little leaven leaveneth the whole lump* (9). Howard reminds us of the English equivalent of this proverb: "One rotten apple will spoil a bushel." Then, he comments: "Wherever men congregate, a misguided, noisy minority can influence a large assembly. Freedom of speech is a precious and inviolate right, but men of every day need to distinguish between claim and proof. . . . But why not apply the proverb positively? A little spiritual leaven can leaven a whole church, community, country, and world. Dare we have such faith?"[8] Paul's warning is followed by an expression of confidence in the Galatians that they will not allow themselves to be further deceived and by a statement on the judgment which will fall upon those who have initiated this deception (10).

Apparently the Apostle was being accused of some inconsistency in preaching and practicing circumcision (11). Perhaps his opponents remembered that he circumcised Timothy the Gentile (Acts 16:3). He did this to avoid criticism from the Jews. It was a principle of Paul's ministry to be "all things to all men" in order to "win some." Thus, he was willing to be a Jew to the Jews (1 Cor. 9:19-23). The argument in verse 11, however, asks why Paul is persecuted by his Galatian opponents if he practices circumcision; that's just what they wanted to do with the Galatians.

Be that as it may, Paul is not about to preach in such a way as to remove *the offence of the cross* (11b). The word *offence* is a translation of the Greek *skandalon* which originally referred to "something which turns out to be a trap, a source of embarrassment and offence, a provocation which arouses resentment and resistance." The Cross is a "stumblingblock" because it proclaims that salvation is provided only through Christ's death. This is resented by the Jews because it invalidates the observance of the Law as a way of salvation. Likewise, it is an offence to the Greeks and Romans because by implication it renders meaningless their extensive religious training. When Christians preached the Cross, they aroused not only thoughts of foolishness in the minds of these people but also feelings of deep resentment (see 1 Cor. 1:21—2:8). Remove this *skandalon* and the Christian message ceases to be authentic and true. To the Corinthians Paul wrote: "I determined not to know any thing among you, save Jesus Christ, and him crucified" (1 Cor. 2:2).

Verse 12 has been interpreted in two ways: (1) suggesting that these agitators of the Galatians mutilate their own bodies and become eunuchs; or (2), that they be cut off from the Galatian community of believers. The first view rests upon a play on words: those who have "cut in" on the Galatians should now "cut off" themselves, presumably by castration. The priests of Cybele, a mythical religion known to the Galatians, practiced this type of emasculation. The second view, which seems more appropriate, reflects the language of Deut. 23:1 ff. That Paul is capable of ordering such action is clear from what he tells the church in Corinth to do with a fornicator in the church (1 Corinthians 5).

Paul is a shepherd with integrity and really does love these Galatians. He will not surrender them to any heretics. He knows that this whole issue is a thrust against the heart of the gospel and if allowed to prevail will destroy their Christian lives. Drastic action is the only acceptable way of saving them and so he commands it. Blessed are the people whose lives are touched by a shepherd with such a heart!

Liberty and Love

Galatians 5:13-15

> 13 For, brethren, ye have been called unto liberty; only use not liberty for an occasion to the flesh, but by love serve one another.
> 14 For all the law is fulfilled in one word, even in this; Thou shalt love thy neighbour as thyself.
> 15 But if ye bite and devour one another, take heed that ye be not consumed one of another.

The loss of freedom is the central concern of the Apostle. But at the same time he recognizes the danger of abusing freedom. *Brethren, ye have been called unto liberty; only use not liberty for an occasion to the flesh, but by love serve one another* (13). Duncan paraphrases: "The door of liberty has been opened, not that through it the desires of the flesh may break out in a riot of selfishness, but that through it there may enter in a new power (to be described later as 'the Spirit') leading us *in love* to a life of mutual service."[9]

1. *Flesh* in this context refers to human nature under the power of sin. Paul uses it here and elsewhere in ways which suggest personification. Adam Clarke defines *flesh* as "all the unrenewed desires and propensities of the mind; whatsoever is not under the influence and guidance of the Holy Spirit of God." Paul is anxious lest an abuse of the believer's freedom, which originally brought deliverance from the compulsive grip and power of sin, might lead back into sin. The word *occasion* (13) in the original language is a military term meaning literally "the starting-point or base of operations for an expedition, then generally the resources needed to carry through an undertaking." The Galatians therefore must be extremely careful not to allow their newfound freedom to become a "starting-point or base of operations" for the inherited sinful nature to take over the life again and become a means of hurting others. Martin's comment is cogent: "The 'flesh' in this

verse means the self-life, still present in the believer and which struggles to re-assert itself—or, to contrive the military metaphor, provides a launching-pad from which sin (as a missile) may be let loose, to the hurt of others."[10]

2. Three groups of religious persons are identifiable in this whole context, especially in chapters 5 and 6: *(a) The libertine,* the free-wheeler who declares that he has been set free in Christ and can live without restraint of any law. His natural inclinations pretty much rule his life. Now that he has been declared acceptable to God through his faith and standing in Christ, he need not give too much attention to the law. This person is also known as an antinomian, the anti-law person. *(b) The legalist,* who is aware of the grace of God but cannot get away from the need to "follow the rules." To be sure, there is a discipline to the Christian life, but that discipline is the outflow of the Spirit's work in the life and is not the life itself. As a matter of fact, living under the Spirit is far more productive of moral rectitude than living according to the rules. When the heart is open to the Spirit, He becomes the loving, yet demanding Teacher of the holy life as exemplified in Christ. Howard makes the point that "the real alternative to the regimentation of legalism is the discipline of the human spirit by submission to the guidance of the Holy Spirit."[11] *(c) The lover of Christ,* who has a deep longing to enjoy and to grow in the Christ-like, life.

> *Oh, to be like Thee! blessed Redeemer,*
> *This is my constant longing and prayer.*
> *Gladly I'll forfeit all of earth's treasures,*
> *Jesus, Thy perfect likeness to wear.*
>
> —Thomas O. Chisholm

3. True faith issuing in liberty issues in community love: *By love serve one another. For all the law is fulfilled in one word, even in this; Thou shalt love thy neighbour as thyself* (13b-14). A new slavery happens in the life of the

believer. The *agape* implanted in the heart binds him not only to God but to his fellow Christians. *Serve* in verse 13 comes from a root which means "to perform the duties of a slave." The welfare of others—material, physical, and spiritual—becomes the concern of the Christian believer and, as Wesley comments, thereby shows that Christ has made him free. When one is liberated in Christ, that kind of benevolent living is heightened. The indwelling Spirit generates the *agape* for a life of true servanthood.

Paul declares that all the law is fulfilled in love to one's neighbor (14; see Lev. 19:18; Mark 12:28-34). This unique truth is also stated in Rom. 13:9, only with a slightly different thrust. *Law* and *fulfilled* are the key words in this Galatians statement. *Law* may refer to (a) the legalism with the works-way of righteousness, or (b) the moral demands upon man's life which arise out of the moral nature of God. *Fulfilled* can either mean (a) "has reached its end or purpose," or (b) "is summed up in," "comprehended in." In the first instance, *fulfilled* suggests that the old way of finding acceptance with God has come to an end and that Christ is the end of the rule of that use of law. In the second instance, it means that love is the only way that one can meet the requirements of the eternal, moral law.

All of the requirements of the law of God can be obeyed only through the divinely implanted love. Thus, the love of Christ spread abroad in the heart is the dynamic for living according to the divine standards. This understanding of the relationship of law and love lies behind the words of Christ: "Think not that I am come to destroy the law, or the prophets: I am not come to destroy, but to fulfil" (Matt. 5:17). Law comes to its fullest expectation of being "lived out" through the indwelling of Christ's love.

Paul sees the possibility of resolving the strife between the Judaizers and the Galatian Christians if love is allowed to prevail among them; else they will destroy one another (15). "Care" is perhaps the best word in modern English for expressing what love really means in neighbor relationships. Paul wants the people in the Galatian churches to start caring for one another and then conflict will cease.

Walking in the Spirit

Galatians 5:16-18

> 16 This I say then, Walk in the Spirit, and ye shall not fulfill the lust of the flesh.
> 17 For the flesh lusteth against the Spirit, and the Spirit against the flesh: and these are contrary the one to the other: so that ye cannot do the things that ye would.
> 18 But if ye be led of the Spirit, ye are not under the law.

"Walk" is the key word in this entire passage. It appears twice (16, 25) and carries the meaning of "conducting one's life in a certain way." In this instance, the word signifies the practical application, in daily conduct, of one's personal communion with God. The use of the term "walk" to express the conduct of the religious man's life is old. Of one of the heroes of the Hebrew faith, the Old Testament records: "Enoch walked with God; and he was not, for God took him" (Gen. 5:24, RSV). Abraham was instructed by God to "walk before me, and be blameless" (Gen. 17:1, RSV).

The *flesh,* the inner sin yet uncleansed, or the idolatrous self-life, is still active in the lives of the readers, constantly raising its ugly head and making demands in its struggle to control their behavior. In fact, the implication is that they are acting in carnal ways, much like the Corinthians, to whom Paul wrote later (1 Cor. 3:1-8). Paul specifically exhorts, *Walk in the Spirit.* The Spirit, referred to here is obviously the divine Spirit, not the human spirit. The human spirit, though majestic in its moral efforts at times, cannot produce the life to which God is calling us. However, as Howard reminds us, Paul is not suggesting an independence between the human and divine spirits. He is referring to the human spirit indwelt by the divine Spirit. "The believer's inner man is thus to be under the motivating, empowering force of the Holy Spirit."[12]

Paul points out the irreconcilable opposites: *The flesh lusteth against the Spirit, and the Spirit against the flesh: and these are contrary the one to the other: so that ye cannot do the things that ye would* (17-18). William Greathouse has said that "this is the most misunderstood verse in the Christian Church." Some within the Church have predicated on this the doctrine of the incessant, hopeless struggle in the believing heart between the flesh and the Spirit. According to them, no hope of deliverance from this conflict can be offered the Christian. Sin is so entwined in man's nature, there is no freedom until he enters heaven. Luther saw the justified Christian as still a sinner. Though forgiven through Christ, every believer inevitably sins, he said, because of the restless power of the flesh which remains until death. Although the flesh is thwarted as we live in the Spirit, full redemption from the heart struggle is impossible in this life. Two mighty forces vie for supremacy in the human soul and "deep settled peace" can never be enjoyed.

This sad state of affairs is much like an experience the author had one time while flying from Kansas City to Denver. The turbulence was very unnerving. I could sense the pilot moving the plane from one altitude to another, apparently hoping to find a smooth airlane. He turned northward for a time and then southward, earnestly seeking for freedom from the wrenching turbulence. Finally, his voice came over the loudspeaker, expressing regret for his failure to locate a calm path for the plane. "Folks," he said, "we have strong north and south winds mixing all over the state of Kansas, and there is no altitude unaffected. I guess we will have to ride it out to Denver. Please fasten your seatbelts." No liberty for us passengers!

It is a false theory that says that we are forever torn between these two equally powerful forces, and thus must live on two levels of life, the higher nature and the lower nature. We may be able periodically through suppression or counteraction to find some peace, but cannot satisfy the human spirit. In this context, that view of Christian experience is a contradiction of Paul's central thought, namely, that in Christ there is freedom from sin, not partial but amazingly complete freedom. The flesh with its desires, its drives to conquer, as an instrument of sin, can be *crucified* (24).

Verse 18 is not an advance on Paul's argument. It simply relates his immediate thought to the issue being addressed in the Epistle: Salvation is by grace, which means freedom from sin by the indwelling, fortifying, cleansing life of the Spirit, and not by works of the law. "But if you are led by the Spirit [present tense, "being led"], you are not under the Law" (18, NASB). Romans 7:4-6 is an excellent commentary on this verse. The law requires moral toil and effort, but all that is involved is human works, which are sinful, because they take their characteristics from the flesh. The presence of the Holy Spirit, on the other hand, brings victory over this bondage to the law and thus to the flesh.

The Harvest of the Spirit

Galatians 5:19-24

> 19 Now the works of the flesh are manifest, which are these; Adultery, fornication, uncleanness, lasciviousness,
> 20 Idolatry, witchcraft, hatred, variance, emulations, wrath, strife, seditions, heresies,
> 21 Envyings, murders, drunkenness, revellings, and such like: of the which I tell you before, as I have also told you in time past, that they which do such things shall not inherit the kingdom of God.
> 22 But the fruit of the Spirit is love, joy, peace, longsuffering, gentleness, goodness, faith,
> 23 Meekness, temperance: against such there is no law.
> 24 And they that are Christ's have crucified the flesh with the affections and lusts.

1. We live either by the Spirit or by the flesh. To build a contrast, Paul, first of all, lists some of the manifestations of the flesh. He gives 15 *works of the flesh* (19-21). This is a representative catalog; he might have added more, as the little phrase in verse 21 suggests: *and such like.* These works fall into four groups (RSV):

a. Sexual vices—fornication, sexual impurity, licentiousness (lack of restraint, abandon).

b. Vices associated with pagan worship—idolatry (perhaps temple prostitution, or worship of images), sorcery (*pharmakeia*, use of drugs for enchantments, magic).

c. Social vices—enmity, strife, jealousy, anger, selfishness, dissension, party spirit, envy (possibly murder).

d. Vices of appetite—drunkenness, carousing.

Every conceivable type of evil can be spawned by the flesh and these evils are totally destructive. Every phase of human existence—physical, material, social, and religious—is affected by them. Someone once commented that the flesh generates sin like the Grand Coulee Dam generates electricity, and sin's power is felt throughout the life of the sinner and his associations just as the elctricity flows through the lines through the northwest and touches the lives of thousands and thousands of people. None of us could argue effectively against the assessment that the age in which we live might well be dubbed "the age of the flesh." Immorality, pornography, obscenity, greed, and endemic strife abound uncontrollably.

Paul draws a very pessimistic picture of the human situation. While he is speaking of the final products of the flesh, he is also reminding us of the depths to which the human heart can fall. We must note also that Paul defines these actions as *works of the flesh.* Some of them are products of the mind and the spirit, not just of the body. Wesley thus comments, "Hence it is clear, the apostle does not by 'the flesh' mean the body, or sensual appetites and inclinations only, but the corruption of human nature, as it spreads through all the powers of the soul, as well as all the members of the body."[13]

Participants in sin of the types mentioned above have no hope of admission into the kingdom of God. *They which do such things shall not inherit the kingdom of God*

(21b). They are not children of God and therefore cannot inherit the Kingdom. Those who belong to God by adoption have an inheritance (see 3:18; Eph. 1:11, 14, 18). The Spirit abiding in, and controlling, their hearts is the "earnest" or "down payment" of that inheritance, namely, full entrance into the New Eden which God has prepared for His family.

2. All who are led by the Spirit enjoy *the fruit of the Spirit* (22-23). In contrast to the works of the flesh, Paul now depicts the fruit of the Spirit, which someone has called "the virtues of Jesus." Several significant features of this catalog of Spirit-inspired virtues are noteworthy.

   a. "They do not represent qualities of personal behavior which one can elect, cultivate, and appropriate as part of one's character," says Betz. "Nor are they 'good deeds' in the sense of Jewish ethics; they do not come from or constitute a code of law which must be obeyed and which can be transgressed."[14] Based on the analogy taken from the cultivation of trees, Paul says they are *fruit,* rather than *works.* Man cannot produce fruit by his own effort; it is created by a power which he does not possess. "Man cannot *make* a fruit."[15] The Spirit is the creator of the fruit, the natural product of the vital relation between the Christian and the Spirit, who creates Christ wihin us. His life is the source of the fruit.

   b. What the Spirit produces in the life is a unity. It is *fruit,* not *fruits,* as we sometimes mistakenly say. The virtues mentioned here are not single gifts of the Spirit (1 Corinthians 12) which nine different persons might possess individually. Rather, each person is to have every virtue. It is not that one person has love and another peace, but every person has a measure of all of them. When the Spirit comes into the heart to dwell in fullness, He produces these manifestations of His presence, in strong contrast to what Betz calls "the open-ended and unstructured list of vices."

   c. Highly provocative is the suggestion that the use of

the singular may indicate that love is the fruit and all the other virtues are particularized expressions of it. This concept fits well with Paul's thought in 1 Cor. 13:13 where he speaks of love as "the greatest gift." In Col. 3:14, he exhorts the Colossians to "put on love, which binds everything together in perfect harmony" (RSV). Love is the all-encompassing spiritual excellence which incorporates all other virtues. Wesley says it is "the root of all the rest." Each fruit defines a certain aspect of love. This has been expressed poetically as follows:

> *Joy is love's cheerfulness.*
>   *Peace is love's confidence.*
>   *Longsuffering is love's composure.*
>   *Kindness is love's considerateness.*
>   *Goodness is love's character.*
>   *Faithfulness is love's constancy.*
>   *Meekness is love's comeliness.*
>   *Self-control is love's conquest.*

d. The Spirit's activity in the believing heart produces a harvest of spiritual qualities which affect the threefold dimension of human life.

(1) The first triad relates to God: love, joy, and peace. These are virtues of the first magnitude, because they are qualities in the nature of the Trinity but they can be generated in the hearts of believers. *Love* is the selfless care which originates in the heart of God and is expressed in the life and death of our Lord. That love can overflow in the heart (Rom. 5:5), and flow out of us to others in redemptive power. *Joy* is delight in God arising out of the reconciliation which He has provided in Christ. *Peace* is the sense of well-being and inner contentment bequeathed by Christ (John 14:27).

(2) The second group of virtues has to do with our relations with others. *Longsuffering,* says Adam Clarke, is "bearing with the frailties and provocations of others, from the consideration that God has borne long with ours."[16] It simply means patience—not going to pieces

when times are tough. *Gentleness* might better be translated "kindness." This is the affection of God for us, and this must be our disposition toward others. When we were sinful, stubborn, rebellious, and careless, God kept on wooing us. We too must be prepared to deal patiently and gently with others in and out of the community of Christ. This quality of spirit does not suggest weakness and sentimentality, because it is tempered with *goodness,* a trait denoting integrity in motivation, manner, and practice. One cannot *be* good and not *do* good. The *being* controls the *doing;* the pure heart produced by the Holy Spirit issues in proper and helpful acts toward others. *Goodness,* based on the meaning of the original language, has a large measure of generosity in it, too.

(3) The first three words relate to God, the second three to our fellowmen, and the third group to ourselves, our character. *Faith* is simply fidelity or trustworthiness. *Meekness* is the antithesis of pride and arrogance. Clarke defines it as "mildness, indulgence toward the weak and erring, patient suffering of injuries without feeling a spirit of revenge, and even balance of tempers and passions, the entire opposite to anger."[17] *Temperance* or "self-control" (the usual modern translation) is the ability to master all one's appetites and passions. Sanders comments that "for the Christian, 'self-control' connotes the subjugation of the self-life in its myriad forms and manifestations, the bringing of the whole nature under the control of the Spirit. It is the outcome not of stern self-repression, but the powerful working of the Spirit within."[18]

e. The fruit of the Spirit stands in direct opposition to, and offers a spiritual answer to, the works of the flesh. For idolatry and sorcery, there is the love of God. For the fear of demons, there is joy and peace. For social strife, there is long-suffering, gentleness, goodness, faithfulness, and meekness. For immorality, impurity, and licentiousness, there is self-control.

f. Against such there is no law (23b) can either be a reference to the virtues listed, or, based on the Greek, to the person practicing these virtues. Ridderbos takes the statement to mean that "the law is not *against* those who walk by the Spirit because in principle they are fulfilling the law (verse 14)."[19] This seems to be the more reasonable explanation. Paul, for sure, would not be suggesting by this statement that the list of virtues constitutes itself a new law. Furthermore, the virtues do not violate any law; in fact, they are expressive of all that was intended by the Law of Moses. We need to keep in mind always, in dealing with instructions on behavior, that the conception of new patterns of living will not automatically bring conformity to them and the corresponding needful ethical responsibility. Motivation and enablement must be given by the Spirit, but the fruit of the Spirit must be cultivated (cf. Phil. 2:12-13). The Spirit possessing the deep recesses of the heart provides the Christian motivation for responsible living.

g. All who truly belong to Christ *have crucified the flesh with the affections and lusts* (24). By identifying with Christ in His death, the believer experiences the death of that recalcitrant element in the flesh known as original sin. Thereby, the flesh no longer acts as an instrument of sin against him. The contradictory power of the flesh is destroyed, and the believer lives in freedom, "according to the Spirit" and not "according to the flesh" (cf. Rom. 8:2-4). The sin principle is expurgated from the inner life and he is free to become what God intended him to be. In response to those teachers who deny the possibility of full deliverance from sin in this life, Howard exclaims, "What a travesty on the gospel when the Cross is made nothing more than sin's competitor, and is even doomed to defeat in the competition! Such a mistaken idea results from a failure to give serious consideration to the crucifixion of the flesh. Jesus died, not to reconcile men to sin, but to deliver them."[20]

Even as born-again believers we must come again to

the Cross and there die to sin if we are to enjoy this free life in the Spirit. A. W. Tozer has well declared:

> There is within the human heart a tough, fibrous root of fallen life, whose nature is to possess, always to possess. . . . There is a veil in our hearts, the veil of our fleshly fallen nature living on, unjudged within us, uncrucified and sin repudiated. . . . It is woven of the fine threads of the self life . . . self-righteousness, self-pity, self-confidence, self-sufficiency, self-adoration, self-love and a host of others like them.[21]

We must invite the Cross to do its full work of putting to death these vestiges of the flesh. Then we will be marvelously free and the fruit of the Spirit will richly grow within us. When the flesh has lost its life, it is no longer able to produce its works in us. And only then can the Spirit do His work of producing the beauty of Christ, who is the essence of holiness.

Life in the Spirit

Galatians 5:25-26

> 25 If we live in the Spirit, let us also walk in the Spirit.
> 26 Let us not be desirous of vain glory, provoking one another, envying one another.

One final exhortation flows from the Apostle's pen. It seems so simple, but upon closer examination it contains a profound truth. *If we live in the Spirit, let us also walk in the Spirit* (25). One might be tempted to think that walking in the Spirit would automatically give life in the Spirit. No, that would be a concession to the false doctrine that Paul has been opposing. *Walking* is possible only by the *living*. Behaving as spiritual people is the result of having a life created by the Spirit. We must always begin at the beginning, which is to surrender to the transforming and cleansing power of the Spirit. Then we can walk—victoriously and winsomely. With the Spirit indwelling us, the fulfillment of the imperative to "walk in the Spirit" is made possible. In this instance, the term "walk" in the original language is a military term, meaning "march," "get in step," "form a line." Paul is suggesting that now that we are living (present tense) in the Spirit, let us "keep in step" with the Spirit. This keeping in step is the moral discipline required of us. It requires us to be good listeners to the instructions of the Spirit which come to us through the written and preached Word, through prayer, and through association with the people of God.

Verse 26 might seem to be out of place, but it serves as a humble reminder of the warning of verse 15, which immediately precedes this long passage on the rivalry between the Spirit and the flesh. If the Galatians are living in the stream of the Spirit, there will be no *vain glory* or boastfulness or the attempt to get ahead of others, which spirit provokes others to envy. The Body of Christ is then splintered, as was the case in Corinth (1 Cor. 1:12-13). Paul concludes that living with the Spirit as the Source of inner spiritual power, the Galatians will become servants to one another and to all men (see v. 13).

Freedom to Serve Others

Galatians 6:1-10

GALATIANS 6

Paul has been speaking of the life in the Spirit, created when we give ourselves fully to the Spirit. He is declaring, at the same time, the norm for the Christian community. Neil says, "He has painted a picture of what the Church would be like if all its members were saints."[1] Now he deals with the Galatians as they really are— something less than saints, as we generally understand that term. Churches are composed of people and people have personal as well as social problems. Jesus knew that struggles would develop in the life of the Church, even between fellow believers, and He gave some instructions as to how to resolve them (see Matthew 18). As recorded in John 17, the Lord's prayer for His disciples and for us, however, focuses on the sanctification of the heart in order that a oneness like unto the unity of the Godhead would be created among His people.

A Faltering Member

Galatians 6:1-5

> 1 Brethren, if a man be overtaken in a fault, ye which are spiritual, restore such an one in the spirit of meekness; considering thyself, lest thou also be tempted.
> 2 Bear ye one another's burdens, and so fulfill the law of Christ.
> 3 For if a man think himself to be something, when he is nothing, he deceiveth himself.
> 4 But let every man prove his own work, and then shall he have rejoicing in himself alone, and not in another.
> 5 For every man shall bear his own burden.

What should be the attitude of the Christian community when one of its members falls into sin? This section provides a most helpful answer.

1. *Overtaken in a fault* (1). The word "overtaken" in the Greek does not refer to a person being discovered committing sin but rather to his being caught unawares by sin in himself, or to his yielding suddenly to a temptation to sin. Stagg suggests that an "unanticipated moral lapse" has occurred. *Fault,* as used in the Authorized Version, is a weak translation. The Greek word means "trespass" or "transgression," indicating a serious moral failure. Jowett paints a vivid picture of this type of person:

> Some evil passion has pounced upon him, and he is broken. Some holy relationship has been snapped, and he is crippled in his moral and spiritual goings. Perhaps his affections have been broken, or his conscience, or his will. Or perhaps he has lost his glorious hope or the confidence of his faith. Here he is, a broken man, the victim of his own broken vows, lame and halt in the pilgrim-way![2]

2. *Gentleness, not judgment.* This person needs help—immediate and loving help. Paul exhorts, *Ye which are spiritual, restore such an one in the spirit of meekness* (1). Who are the "spiritual ones" who are instructed to carry out the restoration? Spirit-filled and Spirit-led members! Paul's view of the state of the church is not a pessimistic one. Several times already he has expressed his belief that the Galatians, like all Christians are under the control of the Spirit to a measure (see 3:2-3, 5, 14; 5:5, 16-18, 22). He does not advocate expulsion or some other severe form of punishment. He calls for sympathy and restoration, rather than criticism. To be free in the Spirit does not mean freedom from responsibility but rather freedom to serve, to become "a Good Samaritan, seeking to restore the cripple to health and strength again."[3]

Restore is a word meaning "repair," as in mending fish nets, or, as Blackwood suggests, "the setting of a bone, as in orthopedic surgery." He comments further:

> Anyone who has endured a fracture knows that setting a bone is a painfilled operation, demanding the finest kind of technical skill from the surgeon. Forgiving and restoring a fractured soul are not easy, either for the one forgiving or the one forgiven. When our own forgiveness has cost God a Cross, need we expect ease and tranquility in our following Christ?[4]

In short, every case of moral failure should be dealt with in a manner that befits spiritual people, that is to say, it should be done *in the spirit of meekness.* "Gentleness" is a good synonym here. Paul is calling for mildness of temper, patience, and nothing that smacks of haughtiness. Jowett's comment is incisive: "The 'touch' of pride is never the minister of healing."[5] The spirit of Jesus is the spirit of meekness. In no way does that suggest spinelessness but rather the strength and stability of wisdom, poise, forthrightness, and dependence upon the resources of the Father.

3. *Individual responsibility.* Paul's words are: . . . *considering thyself, lest thou also be tempted* (1). Here is an

acknowledgment of the fact of the universality of temptation. No Christian can hope to escape temptation. Thus, he must keep his own spiritual life under constant surveillance that Satan not slip up on his "blind side" and take him captive to pride, sensuality, greed, envy, or resentment. It may well be that Paul is suggesting that the very situation of restoring another to the faith can produce subtle temptations of this kind. A steadfast devotement to Christ is our only hope of overcoming temptation (1 Cor. 10:12-13).

4. *Bearing one another's burdens* (2). Given the context in which this majestic word is written, Paul is primarily thinking about the burdens of sin and guilt to which he has just referred. While we Christians are required by love to share other kinds of burdens, these are the burdens we should be most ready to bear. While we must hate sin, we must love the sinner and share his burden of condemnation. Blackwood's word reaches home: "A Christian cannot leave his brother, even his sinful brother, lying humiliated in the dust."[6] We must love and lift with him, in the power of the Spirit, until he is free of his burden. Furthermore, to get under the spiritual load of a brother in the community of believers is an especially effective deterrent against spiritual pride. "If you are inclined to feel proud of your moral or religious superiority to another, try making his weakness and guilt your own burden."[7]

In our burden-bearing we *fulfil the law of Christ*. Law, in this instance, does not mean that Christ has set forth a whole new set of statutes or rules prescribing behavior for all kinds of situations. Loving one's neighbor is commanded, and to the degree that it is required, it is a law. But this is certainly nothing like the law about which Paul has been speaking throughout this Epistle. Christ's law of love is more like a principle of action, a mood and mode of living. It is "the 'life principle' embodied by Christ and to which he called all followers, i.e. the cross as sacrificial service. Christ's love came to ultimate expression in taking on man's burden, even at the cost of his life."[8] When we "get under" another's burden of sin we act out this life principle of Christ, the sacrifice of all for the redemption of the sinner.

5. *Pulling one's own load* (3-5). Paul returns to the matter of personal responsibility and makes three comments important to the sustaining of the life of the Christian community.

 a. Spiritual pride is a form of self-deception (3). When we assist others with their burdens we may be tempted to develop within ourselves "a warm, inner glow of self-satisfaction." As Christians we must always remember that we are sinners saved by grace and grace alone.

 b. One should not compare his spiritual life with that of others; rather, he must examine his own life in relation to that of Christ's. If there is to be any *rejoicing* or "boasting" (NASB), it will not be at the expense of others (4). The NEB translates this verse as follows: "Each man should examine his own conduct for himself; then he can measure his achievement by comparing himself with himself and not with anyone else." There is no place in the Christian community or the Christian's heart for the Pharisaic spirit which proudly declares, "I'm glad I'm not as other men are" (see Luke 18:11).

 c. The exhortation that *every man shall bear his own burden* (5) seems to be in contradiction to what is written in verse 2. The clue is found in the two words used for *burden* in these verses. The word in verse 2 denotes "a crushing load," which is what the guilt of sin becomes. In verse 5 the word is more like "a soldier's pack." Phillips translates this verse as follows: "Every man must 'shoulder his own pack.'" The apparent meaning of this statement is that we must assume responsibility for our own souls before God. The previous verse expresses the Christian's responsibility to the community of believers, while this verse emphasizes his private responsibility. As Howard reminds us, there is an interplay of social and individual responsibility and one must not be emphasized to the exclusion of the other. "In the Christian fellowship the burdens of others are shared in love, but there is also a load that is peculiarly a man's own."[9]

Support of Christian Teachers

Galatians 6:6

> 6 Let him that is taught in the word communicate unto him that teacheth in all good things.

The thought of "bearing burdens" triggered the mind of the Apostle to speak about a related matter. "Let him who is taught the word share all good things with him who teaches" (6, RSV). This note is surprising because one would think Paul would speak about pastors and their provision for daily needs. Evidently, the Early Church had instituted by this time the position of teacher and it was considered a necessary function. With so many Gentiles as well as Jews coming into the Christian fellowship, it was imperative, for their spiritual growth, to instruct them in the faith in some systematic way. The Jewish converts would appreciate a teacher because they had been reared under the rabbis, those splendid teachers of the Jews. Apparently the catechetical function was becoming a full-time assignment and the church was taking on the responsibility of supporting the teachers materially. Good instruction requires diligent study on the part of the teacher. Classroom time must be backed by hours of reading and research.

A church which gives little attention to the teaching of its membership will eventually lose its distinctive ministry through the erosion of faith or through the dilution of the truth by the insidious penetration of heretical concepts. DeWolf's assessment of the need of teaching is cogent:

> We do need preaching to inspire and to win decision. But without solid instruction, decisions for Christ mean little, for the converts know but vaguely who Christ is and can poorly distinguish between the guidance of God and urges of contrary significance. If we magnify the office of teacher in the church, we shall

be acting in accord with the earliest traditions of New Testament Christianity.[10]

We need more than voluntary teachers in the church, too. We must have a corps of full-time, dedicated instructors in our churches and Christian colleges and seminaries to build up the Body of Christ and to keep it vigorous and winsome (see Eph. 4:11-16).

Sowing and Reaping

Galatians 6:7-10

> 7 Be not deceived; God is not mocked: for whatsoever a man soweth, that shall he also reap.
> 8 For he that soweth to his flesh shall of the flesh reap corruption; but he that soweth to the Spirit shall of the Spirit reap life everlasting.
> 9 And let us not be weary in well doing: for in due season we shall reap, if we faint not.
> 10 As we have therefore opportunity, let us do good unto all men, especially unto them who are of the household of faith.

The introduction of this old biblical idea seems out of place at this point, unless we remember the context of the letter. It may be that Paul is returning to the thought in 5:22, where he mentions the fruit of the Spirit, and rounds out that idea in terms of the harvest to come. However, since Paul associates "giving" and "sowing" in other writings, the thought may well have arisen out of the emphasis in verse 6 on sharing one's temporal goods with the teachers. Second Corinthians 9:6 reads: "He who sows sparingly will also reap sparingly, and he who sows bountifully will also reap bountifully" (RSV). This latter view seems most appropriate for interpreting this verse.

1. *God cannot be deceived:* "Make no mistake about this: God is not to be fooled" (7, NEB). Paul warns the Galatians about being deceived by certain teachers among them, but he goes on to remind them that God, by virtue of His infinite knowledge of all things, cannot be deceived. Clarke comments that God "will not permit you to mock him with *pretended* instead of *real* services." You cannot outwit God and finally evade Him.

2. *The law of the harvest is constant.* Paul's maxim here is: *Whatsoever a man soweth, that shall he also reap* (7). "We cannot play fast and loose with the moral order of the universe."[11] The nature of the harvest, it has been said, is determined by the planting: you get what you sow! You cannot reap love and friendship out of greed and stinginess. In a wider sense, if we abuse our newfound freedom in the Spirit and disregard the leading of the Spirit in our daily pursuits, we will pay the penalty sooner or later, namely, bondage. How many of us wish we could roll back the screen of our personal histories and reverse some of our previous decisions! *He that soweth to his flesh shall of the flesh reap corruption; but he that soweth to the Spirit shall of the Spirit reap life everlasting* (8). The consequences of bad sowing are experienced not only in this life but also in the life to come. To sow to the flesh, yielding to one's desires and inclinations in ways not in keeping with the will of God, will bring a final harvest of *corruption,* that is, destruction, death, and total loss. Opposite to corruption is the harvest of *life everlasting,* that consummate life begun in the heart of the believer by the Holy Spirit. Jesus told Nicodemus, "Except a man be born of water and of the Spirit, he cannot enter into the kingdom of God" (John 3:5). All who faithfully sow to the Spirit, that is, appropriate in the life the gifts and graces of the Spirit, will enjoy a final harvest of eternal life. Living and walking in the Spirit is the promise of eternal life.

3. *Perseverance in the practice of good will be rewarded.* The Apostle's exhortation is: *Let us not be weary in well-doing: for in due season we shall reap, if we faint not* (9). Clarke comments that *"well-doing is easier than ill-doing"* but there is always the danger of growing weary because of inward and outward hindrances. Despite the discouragements, we must remember that this is God's world and He will see to it that "we shall reach the fulfillment of our life in the blessedness of his nearer presence."[12] "Don't give

up," Paul writes. "Go on praying, giving, witnessing, sharing, sacrificing; God will not fail you. He will open heaven at last." In effect, the greatest danger confronting "the spiritual farmer," the greatest hindrance to a spiritual harvest, is a fainting heart (Heb. 12:3).

4. *God's time and ours.* "So then, as we have opportunity, let us do good to all men, and especially to those who are of the household of faith" (10, RSV). One of the important words in this verse is "opportunity." In the original language, its literal meaning is "time." It can be translated here: "as we have time" (or occasion). Everyone of us must realize that the times of sharing are under the direction of the Spirit. He will show us these times if we are attuned to His voice. Every time we have to do good to anyone is *our time.*

But God has His time too. In verse 9 Paul wrote that *in due season we shall reap.* In the Greek the word "season" is the same as the word *opportunity,* in verse 10. *In due season* can be translated "in due time" (NASB, NEB), or "in the proper time" (NIV). That little phrase is a reference to the harvesttime, which is *God's time.* God chooses it and we do not know when it will be. However, we know when *our time* is, and that is all we need to know. *God's time* will surely come, so we must take advantage of *our time* to do good to the souls and bodies of men, *especially unto them who are of the household of faith,* since they are our family by faith in our common Lord and thus have a special claim upon us.

Postscript

Galatians 6:11-18

Ordinarily, at this point Paul would simply greet certain persons in the church or send greetings from persons in his company. But that is not the case here. He takes over from his scribe and pens a few concluding words, what we call a P.S. The use of scribes was common in that day. See Paul's reference in Rom. 16:22 to Tertius who served as his scribe for that Epistle. The significant note here is Paul's need to pen "large letters" (NIV), perhaps a reference of some eye problems (11, see 4:12-15). By taking over from his scribe, it may be that Paul wants to summarize his thoughts and thereby show that no distortion has taken place by the hand of his secretary.

The Final Salvo

Galatians 6:11-16

> 11 Ye see how large a letter I have written unto you with mine own hand.
> 12 As many as desire to make a fair shew in the flesh, they constrain you to be circumcised; only lest they should suffer persecution for the cross of Christ.
> 13 For neither they themselves who are circumcised keep the law; but desire to have you circumcised, that they may glory in your flesh.
> 14 But God forbid that I should glory, save in the cross of our Lord Jesus Christ, by whom the world is crucified unto me, and I unto the world.
> 15 For in Christ Jesus neither circumcision availeth any thing, nor uncircumcision, but a new creature.
> 16 And as many as walk according to this rule, peace be on them, and mercy, and upon the Israel of God.

Neil has used this phrase to express Paul's parting shot at the Judaizers. Paul ventures to say that the heart of the problem in the churches in Galatia is simply that these false missionaries are demanding that the Galatian

Christians submit to the Old Testament ceremony of circumcision, and thus certainly be acceptable to God, or be saved. They must demonstrate their commitment to God by this mutilation of the body. Really, Paul says, they desire *to make a fair shew in the flesh* (12) and to *glory in your flesh* (13). Moreover, in his judgment they are "out to save their own skins," for if they insist on circumcision, they will escape the persecution which Paul and his followers have experienced (12) because of their faithful declaration of the saving power of *the cross of Christ*. As long as the Roman government believed that Christianity was a sect of the Jews, the Christians existed in freedom among the Romans. These Judaizers are accused by Paul of seeking protection under that false political shelter.

The final charge is most devastating. Paul says, *Neither they themselves who are circumcised keep the law* (13). He must have known much more about the person or persons involved with this heresy than we know from the letter, else this attack on their motives is unjustified. Needless to say, Christians must exercise utmost control of their thoughts and words when dealing with sticky doctrinal and ethical problems in the Church. We cannot escape the words of our Lord: "Judge not, that ye be not judged" (Matt. 7:1).

One of the grandest verses in all of Scripture breaks forth from the pen of this prince of apostles. "Far be it from me to glory except in the cross of our Lord Jesus Christ, by which the world has been crucified to me, and I to the world (14, RSV).

1. It is not the disposition of Paul to boast in anything or in anyone. In order to have personal satisfaction, he does not need, finally, to win large groups of followers. The Cross is the focus of his life and glory. The reality of all is centered there. The achievements of the Cross are the ultimate source of his satisfaction. Cole summarizes his thoughts as follows: "He could neither boast of being circumcised if he were a Jew, nor of being uncircumcised if

he were a Gentile. The one thing that he can 'boast' about is the cross of Jesus Christ which has made all such distinctions meaningless; for it completely breaks the connection with the old 'outward world' and gives both Jew and Gentile a new perspective."[1]

> *In the cross of Christ I glory,*
> *Tow'ring o'er the wrecks of time.*
> *All the light of sacred story*
> *Gathers round its head sublime.*
>
> —JOHN BOWRING

2. A new creation is all that matters: *In Christ Jesus neither circumcision availeth any thing, nor uncircumcision, but a new creature* (15). This is a familiar Pauline theme, best expressed in 2 Cor. 5:17: "If any one is in Christ, he is a new creation; the old has passed away, behold, the new has come" (RSV). A new creation! The start of a new life! The creation of a new environment, for "grace has changed the world I'm living in"! There is a new company of people to live with! A new perspective on life opens up—a whole new way of looking at everything! All of this is not outward, human display but the outworkings of the power of the Spirit indwelling the life.

3. All who live in keeping with this principle of faith receive the benediction of peace and mercy (16). All such persons constitute the true people of God, *the Israel of God.* This phrase is uniquely Paul's in the New Testament. It recognizes the role of Israel in God's dealing with His sinful creatures, in making preparation for the finished work in Christ. Abraham was the founder of the people of God and we who have come to God by faith in Jesus Christ, Paul has already declared, are participants in that family.

The moral standards of the Old are carried over into the New and Christ has become the meritorious means for living out those standards as the Spirit controls and guides our lives. So Neil concludes: "We are caught up, as Christians, in God's plan for the salvation of the world within the framework of human history. It links us with Moses, Amos, and Isaiah, as much as with the twelve apostles and the saints who succeeded Paul."[2] Faith immerses us in this history through Christ who constitutes within himself the very life and hope of Israel, the people of God.

The Mark of Authenticity

Galatians 6:17-18

> 17 From henceforth let no man trouble me: for I bear in my body the marks of the Lord Jesus.
> 18 Brethren, the grace of our Lord Jesus Christ be with your spirit. Amen.
> Unto the Galatians written from Rome

Paul does not want to be bothered any longer with the Galatian issue. He is confident of his own relationship to Christ. He bears in his body *the marks of the Lord Jesus* (17). *Stigmata* is the Greek word for *marks* and suggests that he is "stigmatized," for everyone knows he belongs to Christ. Against the background of the argument with the Judaizers over circumcision, Paul asserts that the only authentic "body marks" are those scars obtained in suffering for the gospel. Doubtless he remembered the agonizing treatment he received in Lystra when he was stoned and left outside the city for dead (Acts 14:19; see also 2 Tim. 3:11). Paul may have in mind the practice of the pagans in which a mark was branded on the body to show one's commitment to a particular god. Surely Paul had been "branded" as belonging to Christ, but in all likelihood his reference is to the struggle with the Judaizers. He is an open, professing Christian, and his scars are abundant evidence of that fact.

> *Brethren, the grace of our Lord Jesus Christ be with your spirit, Amen* (18).

The Epistle to the
EPHESIANS

Topical Outline of Ephesians

A Christian Greeting (1:1-2)

A Hymn of Salvation (1:3-14)
> The Source and Sphere of Salvation Blessings (1:3)
> Salvation Enacted Before Time (1:4-6)
> Salvation Realized in Time (1:7-14)

A Prayer for Enlightenment (1:15-23)
> The Inspiration for the Prayer (1:15-16)
> The Burden of the Prayer (1:17)
> Seeing with the Eyes of the Heart (1:18-19)
> The Supreme Manifestation of Divine Power (1:20-23)

The Creation of a New People (2:1-22)
> Salvation by Resurrection (2:1-10)
> One Body in Christ (2:11-22)

A Prayer for Divine Fullness (3:1-21)
> Paul's Stewardship of the Mystery (3:1-13)
> The Petition for Divine Fullness (3:14-21)

The Unity of the Church (4:1-16)
> The Call to Unity (4:1-6)
> Diversity in Unity (4:7-16)

The Old Life and the New (4:17-32)
> Life Without Christ (4:17-19)
> Life with Christ (4:20-24)
> New-Life Injunctions (4:25-32)

Living as the Beloved (5:1-21)
> Walking in Love (5:1-7)
> Walking in Light (5:8-14)
> Walking in Wisdom (5:15-21)

Christian Relationships (5:22—6:9)
> The Relationship of Husbands and Wives (5:22-33)
> The Relationship of Parents and Children (6:1-4)
> The Relationship of Masters and Slaves (6:5-9)

Introduction

A serious student of Paul's writings has difficulty deciding whether the Epistle to the Romans or the Epistle to the Ephesians has been more influential in molding Christian thought in the history of the Church, and especially in our times. Romans played an important role in the personal lives and in the seminal writings of Augustine, Luther, Wesley, and Karl Barth. However, Ephesians has broken loose the deepest springs of appreciation and commitment from some of Christendom's great leaders. It has been said that John Calvin's favorite book was Ephesians and that John Knox, the great Scottish Reformer, while he lay on his deathbed, frequently had Calvin's sermons on Ephesians read to him. It is no wonder, then, that Armitage Robinson called it "the crown of St. Paul's writings," and Samuel Taylor Coleridge "the divinest composition of man."

Only heaven will reveal the countless numbers of persons who have come to a satisfying faith through the preaching and reading of this majestic Epistle. John Mackay, longtime president of Princeton Theological Seminary, once wrote, "To this book I owe my life." Through reading Ephesians he came to a vital experience of saving grace, about which he wrote later: "Everything was new. . . . I had a new outlook, new experiences, new attitudes to other people, I loved God. Jesus Christ became the centre of everything. The only explanation I could give to myself and to others was in the words of the Ephesian

Letter. . . . My life began to be set to the music of that passage which begins 'And you hath he quickened who were dead in trespasses and sins' (2:1)."[2]

Authorship

In two places in the Epistle the writer identifies himself as Paul the Apostle (1:1; 3:1). Nineteenth century New Testament liberal thought was skeptical about the Pauline authorship of Ephesians but many scholars today still hold to the early view that Paul was the author. Ignatius of Antioch, Polycarp of Smyrna, Irenaeus of Lyons, Clement of Alexandria, and Tertullian of Carthage are to be included on the list of the Early Church Fathers who believed the letter to be genuinely Pauline. In the 20th century, such eminent teachers as Markus Barth, William Barclay, Donald Guthrie, B. F. Westcott, J. Armitage Robinson, F. F. Bruce, A. M. Hunter and C. H. Dodd consider it to be a product of the pen of Paul. The conclusion of F. F. Bruce is worth pondering: "The man who could write Ephesians must have been the apostle's equal, if not his superior, in mental stature and spiritual insight. . . . Of such a second Paul early Christian history has no knowledge."[1]

Time and Place of Composition

The important clue to the questions of the time and place of writing is the reference to imprisonment in the Epistle (3:1; 5:1; 6:20). The Book of Acts offers evidence that the Apostle was in prison in Philippi (16:23 ff.), in Caesarea (24:27), and Rome (28:16 ff.). In 2 Cor. 11:23 Paul also tells us of having been "in prisons more frequent." Some suggestions appear in his writings to the effect that he may have been in prison in Ephesus, but the evidence of incarceration there is not strong. In all likelihood Ephesians was written from Rome where Paul was imprisoned and where he also composed Colossians, Philemon, and probably Philippians, this quartet comprising the "Prison Epistles." A date of A.D. 60 or 61 would thus be appropriate.

Recipients of the Letter

The title, which has been attached to the letter from the earliest centuries, simply says, "To the Ephesians." However, the best and earliest manuscripts omit the phrase *at Ephesus* in 1:1. Because Paul does not greet friends at the conclusion of the Epistle and does not seem to know the readers (1:15; 3:2; 4:20-21), it has been concluded that the letter was not written primarily to the church at Ephesus. Among the several theories regarding this discrepancy, the most reasonable one states that the Epistle was not addressed to a particular church but served as a circular letter to all the churches of Western Asia. Originally, a blank space was left at the place where *at Ephesus* appears in order that other church names could be inserted. However, later on, because Ephesus was the principal church in the region and possibly had received the letter first, the name of Ephesus became the permanent identification for the letter. Probably Tychicus delivered the letter at the same time he delivered the Epistle to the Colossians as well as the short note to Philemon. The similarity of language between Colossians and Ephesians abundantly supports this view. Also, Philemon, the Christian slave owner, lived in Colosse.

The Theme of the Epistle

Paul's central theme is the reuniting of all things to God through Christ Jesus. The pre-Creation, redemptive plan of God was designed to this end. A deep rift exists at the heart of things and it includes the tragic alienation of man and the cosmos from the Creator. Discord is the most characteristic trait of man's life and the world around him. Through the ministry of Christ, which is the historical actualization of His eternal purpose, God has moved into this disharmony to correct it. A key verse is 1:10: "That in the dispensation of the fulness of times he [God] might gather together in one all things in Christ, both which are in heaven, and which are on earth." Christ's work of unity begins with the change of the hearts of men. Being "in Christ" is one of Paul's ways of expressing this transformation. To be "in Christ" means to be adopted into the family of God (1:5), to be forgiven of sins (1:7), to be sealed with the Holy Spirit (1:13), to be resurrected from spiritual deadness (2:1-6), to be reconciled to God (2:13-18), to have put on the robe of righteousness (4:22-24), to have experienced holiness (3:14-21), and to have begun to lead ethically and socially sensitive lives (cc. 5—6).

As a continuing instrument of reconciliation and unity, God has created the Church, which is Christ's Body. Jews and Gentiles become one in the Body of Christ (2:13-18). All barriers thus have been broken down between God and man and between man and his fellowmen. When the Church is *really* the Church, she functions in unity like a household, and like a political unit where all citizens have equal rights, and becomes a holy temple in which the Holy Spirit dwells (2:19-20). Christ is the Head of the Church and He gives to her all the graces and gifts necessary for the Church's growth and evangelization of the world (4:1-16). Made holy and blameless by the sanctifying power of the Spirit, the Church lives as the divine model of peace and unity before all the world.

A Christian Greeting

Ephesians 1:1-2

Ephesians 1:1-2

> 1 Paul, an apostle of Jesus Christ by the will of God, to the saints which are at Ephesus, and to the faithful in Christ Jesus:
> 2 Grace be to you, and peace, from God our Father, and from the Lord Jesus Christ.

When we move from Galatians to Ephesians we are conscious of entering an entirely different atmosphere. As G. G. Findlay comments, "We leave the region of controversy for that of meditation. From the battle-field we step into the hush and stillness of the temple. . . . It is as though a door were suddenly opened in heaven; it shuts behind us, and earthly tumult dies away."[1] All who spend any time in this brief Epistle will readily testify that it feeds the soul and uplifts the spirit in ways unlike any other writing of Paul. It breathes peace and hope, and leaves the explorer of its truth with a sense of victory.

The salutation in verses 1 and 2 is typical of letters in Paul's day. It was usual for the name of the writer to be given first, then the readers identified, and finally the greeting expressed. Paul, however, always gives the salutation a distinctively Christian flavor and at the same time varies it according to the circumstances of the people to whom he is addressing the letter.

1. *God's Ambassador. Paul calls himself an apostle of Jesus Christ by the will of God* (1a). He makes two assertions in this statement. First, he is an *apostle,* and, second, he is such *by the will of God.*

a. The term "apostle" derives from the Greek *apostolos,* and literally means "sent one." In this basic sense the term is used of all Christian missionaries. All of God's workmen have an apostolic relationship and responsibility; that is to say, they are messengers or ambassadors, sent on a mission of redemption for the Lord. However, Paul probably is thinking in more restrictive terms in writing of his own apostleship. When he speaks of himself as *an apostle of Jesus Christ* he may very well be saying that he belongs in that select company of messengers, like the Twelve, who were specially related to the Master. For, after all, he had been directly and personally commissioned by Christ to preach the gospel, as the Damascus Road conversion accounts make clear (see Acts 26:15-23; Galatians 1—2).

b. Paul's apostleship was a creation of *the will of God.* The sense of ambassadorship, carrying the good news to a lost world, came neither by a pronouncement of the Early Church and the 12 apostles nor by any spiritual merit of his own, but by a direct action of God. R. W. Dale comments that Paul means the divine will was "the strong yet gracious force which placed him in the apostleship, and which sustained him in all his apostolic labors and sufferings."[2]

The ministry of the Church must rest upon the sense of being on a special mission for God. If it does not, there is the possibility and probability of defection. The saving truth must be delivered and we, clergy and laity together, the entire body of believers, must be caught up in the urgency of proclaiming and witnessing to God's redeeming grace. We are God's ambassadors, and because we have been commissioned by the will of God, we are part of the divine master plan of reconciling a lost world to God (2 Cor. 5:20).

2. *God's people. Paul addresses his letter to the saints which are at Ephesus, and to the faithful in Christ Jesus* (1b). Three significant notes are found in this characterization.

a. The recipients of this letter are *saints.* In what sense are they saints? This title is an equivalent of the title "Christian." Everyone who receives Christ into his life is, at the same time, initially sanctified, the guilt of committed sins being cleansed away and the old life ended. The reception of the Spirit in this initial experience of grace makes us "holy ones" before God. Sainthood is not reserved for the "wholly sanctified" or a special group of super Christians. Furthermore, the life to which the converted is called is no different in ethical demand from the life to which those who enjoy the full blessings of salvation are called. The sanctity of the saved person is not merely a matter of new standing with God; it is also a reality of the inner spirit which is lived in a new, dynamic relationship with God through Christ.

b. These readers are called *the faithful in Christ Jesus.* The term *faithful* in the original language can be translated either "faithful ones" (loyal ones) or "believers." Both ideas are encompassed in the word. They are believers in Christ and they are faithfully following Him. The act of believing issues in fidelity. Constant obedience to and trust in Christ produce the grace of fidelity.

c. The recipients of the letter live *at Ephesus.* Interestingly, this phrase *at Ephesus* does not appear in the earliest and best manuscripts of the New Testament. It may well be that Paul left a blank space so that each church in the western part of Asia Minor where the letter circulated could insert its own name. Since Ephesus was the chief city of that region, and probably the church there received the letter first, it gave its name to the Epistle. Being more of a homily than a letter, this theory seems reasonable.

3. *God's blessing.* Paul writes: *Grace be to you, and peace, from God our Father, and from the Lord Jesus Christ* (2). Acting as God's messenger, he pronounces the divine blessings: *grace* and *peace.* Grace encompasses all the providential acts of God on our behalf, initiating and sustaining in us a saving relationship with himself. It is His free and loving favor toward us, even when we did not deserve it. Peace is the consequence of enjoying the grace of God. It signifies the cessation of strife in the heart created by sin, and the deep sense of spiritual wholeness, soundness and contentment which invades the spirit. Summers comments: "Sin and conscience, like twin hunters, hound man in his life and his attempt to do what is right. Grace and peace defeat these hunters. Grace takes care of the problem of sin; peace takes care of the problem of conscience."[3]

God our Father and *the Lord Jesus Christ* together constitute the Source of these blessings. Out of the loving heart of the fatherly God has come the provision of grace and peace, and by the mediation of Christ these salvation blessings have been realized in our lives.

A Hymn of Salvation
Ephesians 1:3-14

In one long sentence embracing all these verses the apostle Paul gives us "one of the most sublime of inspired utterances" in all of Holy Writ. It is, as Findlay has commented, "a magnificent gate" into the realm of grace which challenges all our interpretative powers to expose. "Standing with the men of his day, the new-born community of the sons of God in Christ, midway between the ages past and to come, he [Paul] looks backward to the source of man's salvation when it lay a silent thought in the mind of God, and forward to the hour when it shall have accomplished its promise and achieved our redemption" (see also 2:7; 3:5, 21; Col. 1:26).[1]

This majestic passage has often been referred to as a doxology, a literal explosion of praise to God on the part of the author as he contemplates what lies behind all that has happened in his life and in the lives of his readers. John Wick Bowman once called it "a hymn of salvation." It relates how God laid the plans for man's redemption and how those plans are being fulfilled and actualized in the hearts and lives of these first-century Christians and will be realized also in the lives of all who have been and are responding since that early day. The history of salvation seems to be the essence of this exuberant testimony.

The Source and Sphere of Salvation Blessings

Ephesians 1:3

> 3 Blessed be the God and Father of our Lord Jesus Christ, who hath blessed us with all spiritual blessings in heavenly places in Christ:

These words call to mind a Psalm of David:

> Bless the Lord, O my soul;
> and all that is within me, bless his holy name!
> Bless the Lord, O my soul,
> and forget not all his benefits,
> who forgives all your iniquity,
> who heals all your diseases,
> who redeems your life from the Pit,
> who crowns you with steadfast love and mercy,
> who satisfies you with good as long as you live
> so that your youth is renewed like the eagle's.
>
> —Ps. 103:1-5, RSV

No doubt, Paul had been reared spiritually on such doxological passages from the old Scriptures, and especially this one because it was a praise to God for His care of the people of Israel at the time of their deliverance from Egypt.

1. *Blessed* is a priceless word in the Scripture and it defies

full definition. It has been suggested that this word may carry in itself the central theme of all the Bible. In the New Testament this unique word is used only of God, never of man or any other creature. Taken from the Greek *eulogētos,* a compound word composed of *eu,* meaning "well" and *logētos,* meaning "speaking," it bears the idea of "speaking well" or "eulogizing." In effect, the Apostle is saying literally, "Let's eulogize God," or, "Let's speak well of our God," or, "Let's say good things about our God."

While many things praiseworthy may be spoken about God, such as His constancy in love, in mercy, and unimpeachable motives, the important truth is that He is the *Father.* The Supreme One is not an austere, capricious judge of mankind but the Eternal Father—loving, merciful, and tender in spirit like Christ. Moreover, the One who deserves our praise is the One whom Christ revealed to us as His Father. In His high priestly prayer (John 17) Jesus spoke clearly of His relationship to the Father as Son and the expectation that we who believe and receive His sanctifying grace will be more deeply conscious of that relationship: "As thou, Father, art in me, and I in thee, so also may they be in us, that the world may believe that thou didst send me" (John 17:21, NEB).

2. *Blessed us.* Our blessing of God is our response to the blessings of salvation which have come from His hand. Our "speaking" may not change things but God's "speaking" indeed does. His word is creative, a unit of power; it brings into existence that which does not exist. We praise Him for His magnificent work in fashioning our world but nothing He has done or continues to do in the natural order matches the beauty of a spiritually newborn child. The announcement of forgiveness to our sin-weary souls exceeds our finite comprehension, but we know when it happens. It is sheer miracle and we cannot but praise Him.

3. *With all spiritual blessings.* This phrase in the original language is singular, so we should translate it: "with every spiritual blessing," or "with every possible benefit in

Christ" (Phillips). Paul does not have in mind all the material and physical blessings which originate with God, but more specifically the spiritual benefits which come to us through the Spirit. "Whatever our spiritual lives require, God amply and abundantly provides."[2] However, the enjoyment of the new life through the Spirit develops in us a new appreciation of all the material, physical, and intellectual blessings.

4. *In heavenly places in Christ.* This rare phrase, literally, "in the heavenlies," appears only in Ephesians (1:3, 20; 2:6; 3:10; 6:12). A similar thought is expressed in Phil. 3:20 where Paul asserts, "Our commonwealth is in heaven" (RSV). While the meaning of the phrase is different in the other references in Ephesians, here it designates the sphere in which the spiritual blessings are experienced. It speaks of the realm of spiritual experience to which the believer has been lifted in Christ. Vaughn writes, "It speaks not of the heaven of the future but of the heaven that lies within and around the Christian here and now. Believers do indeed belong to two worlds (Phil. 3:20)."[3] The inner life of the believer has been invaded by the power of heaven. He possesses eternal life, the life of heaven, and is, therefore, uniquely a resident of the kingdom of heaven. He is lifted above the earthly, the worldly, and the temporal. Now, of course, he is *in* the world but not *of* the world (see John 17:13-16).

In Christ is one of Paul's important concepts. It appears scores of times in a variety of forms in his writings. The blessings of God, for which we give praise continually, are actualized in the believer in the relationship with Christ. To speak of "being in Christ" is not to declare a strange, quasi-physical union, as the religious pagans of Paul's day preached. Nevertheless, the union with Christ is mystical in nature, as mystical as the union which exists between a man and woman in a loving marriage.

Life in its many dimensions is totally shared together. There are dependencies as well as freedoms but in a sense there is "one life." So it is with being "in Christ." He creates the spiritual realm in which believers exist. He defines the spiritual boundaries of it and provides the bases for joy and peace. In this relationship we contribute trust and obedience, and Christ administers grace and peace.

Salvation Enacted Before Time

Ephesians 1:4-6

> 4 According as he hath chosen us in him before the foundation of the world, that we should be holy and without blame before him in love:
> 5 Having predestinated us unto the adoption of children by Jesus Christ to himself, according to the good pleasure of his will,
> 6 To the praise of the glory of his grace, wherein he hath made us accepted in the beloved.

The blessings which accrue to God's people are not accidental; they are created by God and represent the fulfillment of His purposes established in His mind *before the foundation of the world* (4). Our salvation is not an afterthought, brought on by the fall of mankind into sin. It was rooted in the eternal will of God. Robinson comments, "In eternity it is not new; though in time it appears as new."[4]

1. The eternal purpose or will of God is that *we should be holy and without blame before him* (4; see Col. 1:22). Here we touch the great goal of God's redemptive plan. Holiness and blamelessness are two aspects of the transforming grace of God in the life. *Holy* expresses more than separation unto God's service, though that surely is of the essence of holiness. More specifically it speaks of the inner, moral difference which prevails when God's grace is operative in the heart of the believer. *Blameless* or "spotless" is a concept taken from the sacrificial system of Israel which required that animals presented for offerings be without blemish (Lev. 1:3, 10).

For Paul, however, the word takes on an exacting ethical meaning. Later on in this Epistle Paul will speak of Christ offering himself in death in order that the Church, the bride, might be sanctified and be presented as "not having spot, or wrinkle, or any such; but that it should be holy and without blemish" (5:25-27). The man in Christ can be without blemish "not merely by human standards but *before Him* who is Witness of all that a man does, and thinks, and says."[5] Christ is the blameless Lamb who is offered up for our complete cleansing, that is, that we may be holy and without blemish (Heb. 9:14).

Holy might well be seen as the inner spiritual quality, whereas *without blame* may refer to the outer conduct of life. These traits of holiness and blamelessness are to have the distinctive attribute of love. Clarke comments that *"love* must fill their hearts towards God and each other, and *love* must be the *motive* and *end* of all their *words* and *works."*[6]

2. Election speaks of God's way of actualizing His purpose of salvation. Two words in this passage are critical to this idea, namely *chosen* (4) and *predestinated* (5). The word *chosen* is taken from a root meaning "selected" or "called out from a group," thus, the idea of election. This concept of God calling and choosing sinners for salvation is a major New Testament teaching. The Greek word translated *predestinated* here means literally "marked off in advance" or "determined beforehand." These two words carry essentially the same meaning, that is to say, they relate to the same divine act. God has *chosen* individuals out of the group of men and predestined them for His salvation.

Several truths must be kept in mind in dealing with divine election.

First, it is intended to emphasize that God has taken the initiative in bringing about our redemption. The entire chapter speaks not of any sinister act on the part of God to separate mankind into two groups, those destined to salvation and those destined to perdition. Love and mercy toward all persons undergirds all that is said in this chapter. Barth writes: "Eph. 1 bears testimony to the living God, the Father, the Son, and the Spirit. Everything said is personal, intimate, functional. An invitation to fatalism under the scheme of double predestination or another deterministic plan cannot be found here."[7]

Second, the election of God is not arbitrary, so that some persons are the beneficiaries of grace and others are not. Salvation is extended to all men, as the Bible makes abundantly clear (John 3:16; Rom. 1:16; 10:13). The elect are constituted, not by absolute decree without respect to human decision, but by acceptance of the conditions of God's call by the person. John Mackay is correct when he writes: "To be 'chosen in Christ,' means, therefore, to be chosen to be saved by one who excludes no one who comes to Him. None are cut off from God's election in Christ but those who deliberately cut themselves off."[8]

Third, God's foreknowledge is not causative. We are not without freedom because He already knows our actions. However, a person knows at the time of his conversion that he has made a choice for Christ, but as he reflects more and more on his experience, he realizes that "even those very first stirrings in his own heart which led him to choose Christ were the work of the Holy Spirit."[9]

Fourth, the key phrase in this discussion is *in him* (4). It is especially important because it explicitly states the sphere in which redemption through election is fulfilled and realized. *Christ is the provisional realization of the choice of God,* and as Dale notes, "We are all among the non-elect until we are in Him. But once in Christ we are caught in the currents of the eternal purposes of the divine love."[10]

Fifth, the Church is composed of the elect or called-out ones, the *ecclesia.* Christ himself is "the first elect," the First upon whom the Father has set His favor, and all who relate to Christ are with Him the elect, the Church.

The doctrine of election is another way of speaking of God's eternal involvement with us to effect our salvation. Because He loves us, He chooses us in Christ, He foreordains us to adoption or sonship through the work of His beloved Son.

3. Election and predestination result in our *adoption* into the family of God. *Adoption* was a common practice in the Roman world at that time, and some scholars have determined that it was also practiced by some Jewish sects. It is a legal term and refers to the practice of taking a person from outside the family and bringing him into the family and granting him all the privileges and inheritance of the family. God calls the sinner, the outsider, and graciously brings him into His divine family. Notice the Scripture says, *adoption of children by Jesus Christ to himself* (5). *To himself* makes clear that God himself is the One with whom believers enjoy a filial relationship through adoption.

Furthermore, this new relationship with God is *according to the good pleasure of his will,* which is to emphasize the fact that the choice of God finally is not generated in us by our own efforts but arises out of His own goodness and will. Bruce interprets this phrase as follows: "It was not because he foreknew that we would believe the gospel, that He singled us out for such an honour as this. The ground must be sought exclusively in His own gracious character."[11]

4. All this redeeming activity of God has been done *to the praise of the glory of his grace* (6). This beautiful clause appears three times in this hymn of salvation (6, 12, 14) and is designed to turn us into praiseful people. We tend to want to center our thoughts on the *benefits* which God's grace has brought to us; rather we should focus on praise of the *Giver*. The purpose of our lives is to praise God (Isa. 43:21; Matt. 5:15-16).

God has moved into our wretched lives to redeem them that we might have fellowship with Him and to tell all the world the greatness of His love and grace. Perhaps, at times, in our humanness we bog down in our efforts to "save a lost world," but failure and disappointment lie down that road. It is God's work to save; it is ours to "sing His praises, to bless His name." In remarkable ways that kind of testimony opens door to the ministry of grace in the lives of others.

Salvation Realized in Time

Ephesians 1:7-14

> 7 In whom we have redemption through his blood, the forgiveness of sins, according to the riches of his grace;
> 8 Wherein he hath abounded toward us in all wisdom and prudence;
> 9 Having made known unto us the mystery of his will, according to his good pleasure which he hath purposed in himself:
> 10 That in the dispensation of the fulness of times he might gather together in one all things in Christ, both which are in heaven, and which are on earth; even in him:
> 11 In whom also we have obtained an inheritance, being predestinated according to the purpose of him who worketh all things after the counsel of his own will:
> 12 That we should be to the praise of his glory, who first trusted in Christ.
> 13 In whom ye also trusted, after that ye heard the word of truth, the gospel of your salvation: in whom also after that ye believed, ye were sealed with that holy Spirit of promise,
> 14 Which is the earnest of our inheritance until the redemption of the purchased possession, unto the praise of his glory.

Paul has spoken of the work of the Father in salvation; now he turns to speak of the saving activity of the Son. What had been planned before time is being realized in mankind's history, in the lives of persons and in the Church. Five major thoughts surface in this statement concerning the now-time, saving activity of the *beloved.*

1. *Redemption through Christ's blood* (7a). The key word in this clause is *redemption.* It is a metaphor from the slave markets of the ancient world. A person could gain freedom for a slave by making a payment in his behalf, in other words, offering a ransom for him. Unregenerate humanity is caught in the slavery of sin, "sold under sin," to use a Pauline term, but Christ has offered himself in death at the Cross as a ransom for mankind.

Jesus himself so described His ministry: "The Son of man also came not to be served but to serve, and to give his life as a ransom for many" (Mark 10:45, RSV).

"Ransom" suggests that payment was paid to someone for our release from sin. Perhaps a better interpretation is that Christ's death was the "costly price" paid for our deliverance. The sufferings of Christ were substituted for the punishment rightfully due us, and God's acceptance of His Son's substitution enabled Him to forgive our sins. We are thus granted release from the bondage of sin.

Through his blood cannot be construed to mean only a life given up for someone else's life; it denotes the acceptance of death as a sacrifice, the benefits of which accrue to others. This is "the price of immeasurable costliness." Fanny Crosby understood Paul's word when she wrote:

> *Redeemed—how I love to proclaim it!*
> *Redeemed by the blood of the Lamb!*
> *Redeemed through His infinite mercy,*
> *His child, and forever, I am.*

2. *The forgiveness of sins* (7b). Forgiveness includes also our consciousness of redemption. Paul's usual word for forgiveness carries the idea of "showing favor" or "being gracious" to another. But here he uses a word which means "letting go," "not exacting payment," or "setting aside." When God forgives, according to Paul, He does not exact payment for sins committed, that is, He does not demand the just punishment. Why? Because Christ has paid the price for us! So Dale writes, "When God forgives He actually remits our sin. Our responsibility for it ceases. The guilt of it is no longer ours. That He should be able to give us this release is infinitely more wonderful than that He should be able to kindle the fires of the sun and to control, through age after age, the courses of the stars."[12]

The forgiveness of our trespasses—our false steps, deviations from the divine law, misdeeds—results from God's grace. What God performs in the believing heart is in conformity with His grace; it is in keeping with what He did at Calvary when He removed the barriers to His free acceptance and reconciliation of His creatures who dare to believe in Him. The cross of Christ exposes *the riches of his grace.* "God's giving is not merely out of those *riches* but *according to* their measure."[13] Out of the experience of forgiveness comes not only the consciousness of the forgiveness of sins but also the necessary wisdom and insight to understand God's purposes and to conduct one's life accordingly (8).

3. *The uniting of all things in Christ* (9-10). Faith is a way of knowing. A revelation attends the experience of grace. The forgiven heart, the child adopted into the heavenly family, gains a new perspective on God's purposes. *The mystery of his will* is unlocked (see also 3:3-4, 9; 5:32; 6:19). He knows what God is all about. For the nonbeliever all is a mystery, but for the believer the mystery has become "an open secret." What is "God's unveiled secret"? Bruce decides it is "the establishment of a new order, a new creation, of which Christ is the acknowledged head."[14] God's grand purpose is to unite *all things in Christ, both which are in heaven, and which are on earth; even in him* (10). Since the fall of mankind, this world has been in disarray, fractured, and incapable, by any inherent powers, to put itself together. But God intends to do just that through Jesus Christ.

To *gather together in one* is expressed in the original language by an unusual word. It means literally "to bring to a head." In those days it was used to indicate the addition of a series of numbers, that is, "to add up a sum." The verb was also used to designate the summary at the end of an essay. Also, the plaiting of strands of cord to make a rope was expressed by this verb. So, the word as used here is highly suggestive. God intends "to head everything up" in Christ. Or, He purposes to bring together all the loose strands of cosmic and human existence caused by sin and bind them into a peaceful unity. As Foulkes comments, "Paul seems to picture all . . . of God's possessions as having been scattered in the conflict with the forces of evil. It was his purpose that he would gather up all these scattered holdings and put them under one supreme captain, Jesus Christ."[15]

From this concept of unity we are not to assume a universalism, which asserts that ultimately everybody will be saved. The teachings of the Bible will not support such a doctrine. All that Paul means here is that "one day God's universe, into which sin has brought such disorder and confusion, will be restored to harmony and unity under the headship of Christ."[16]

4. *An inheritance* (11-12). Paul's sense of history breaks through every now and then and it offers fresh insights into the gospel. Here the concept of having an inheritance, so precious to the Hebrew understanding of their relationship to God, adds to the meaning of salvation. Notice, first, that Paul uses the first person plural ("we") in verses 11-12. The reference would appear to be to the Christian Jews who saw in Christ the fulfillment of the Messianic prophecies and who accepted Him as such. Paul himself is in that group. The conversion of the Jews was the first step in the realization of God's purpose to unite all things in Christ (10). The second stage is implied in verses 13-14 where Paul shifts to the use of the second person plural ("ye"), apparently referring to the Gentile Christians. They now are included in God's grand purpose.

The clause *in whom also we have obtained an inheritance* can either mean that in receiving Christ they became heirs of the blessings of salvation or they became God's heritage, that is, they are now God's special possession. Both ideas have rootage in the Old Testament which records that Israel received the land of Canaan as an inheritance but also that Israel became God's inheritance. Deuteronomy 32:9 (NIV) reads: "The Lord's portion is his people, Jacob his allotted inheritance." This latter idea seems to be the proper one. The old Israel was God's heritage; the new Israel, the Church, is likewise His heritage. Both Jew and Gentile must come to Christ if they are to share in this relationship, for the old order is gathered up in the new (see 1 Pet. 2:9—"God's own people," RSV; Exod. 19:5-6).

5. *Sealed with the Holy Spirit* (13-14). Turning now to the Gentile Christians to whom he is writing, the Apostle identifies three stages in their Christian pilgrimage.

First, they *heard the word of truth, the gospel of your salvation* (13a). The "gospel" is the good news that God has provided full redemption, not through human good works, but through faith in Christ Jesus. Christ is the center of the gospel—what He is and what He did is the *truth.* The Gentiles received this gracious message through gospel preaching. Hearing is the first stage (see Rom. 10:14).

Second, they *believed* in Christ (13b). After hearing comes believing. Faith is trustful and obedient response to the call of God in Christ Jesus. Faith is not "blind faith"; it has content and that content is Christ. The call is to come to Christ; believing is the act of embracing Christ as Lord.

Third, they *were sealed with that holy Spirit of promise* (13c). Already Paul has talked about the ministry of the Father and the Son; now he speaks of the work of the Holy Spirit. The original language here suggests a deeper relationship with God. It literally says, "In whom [Christ] also having believed [a completed action], you were sealed with the Holy Spirit." This implies that the sealing was not concurrent with the initial believing but followed it as a distinct experience. "Sealing" refers to a current process of identification and certification by which, for example, letters, contracts, and official papers were first fastened with a blob of warm wax into which the signer pressed his signet ring or stone, thereby identifying the owner and certifying its contents.

Two thoughts concerning the ministry of the Holy Spirit in the believer's heart are intended by this metaphor. First, to be sealed means to be attested or declared genuine. John Wesley says that the sealing implies "a full impression of the image of God on their souls."[17] Second, to be sealed by the Holy Spirit means to be possessed or owned entirely by the Spirit. Ralph Earle comments, "When a person surrenders himself completely to Christ, to belong wholly to Him and no longer to be his own property, then he is 'sealed' with the Holy Spirit as a sign that he belongs no more to himself, but to God."[18]

The Holy Spirit is the *Spirit of promise,* announced by the prophets of the old dispensation (Ezek. 36:26 ff; 37:1-14; Joel 2:28 ff) and by our Lord (Luke 24:49; Acts 1:4-5, 8) and poured out on the Day of Pentecost upon the believing disciples (Acts 2:1-4, 17, 33, 39). Moreover, the Holy Spirit is *the earnest of our inheritance until the redemption of the purchased possession* (14). *Earnest* has been variously translated: "advance payment" (Goodspeed), "pledge" (NASB), "deposit" (NIV). Obviously, the thrust of this concept is toward the future. The partial payment or deposit is a guarantee of full payment later.

What God has given in the release of His Spirit in our hearts is a guarantee that a fuller measure will be released to us when He takes us into His kingdom eternally. Being filled with the Holy Spirit is a foretaste of the inexpressible joy and peace into which we will enter one day. The phrase *the redemption of the purchased possession* reinforces the truth expressed in verse 11. We are God's possession, now that we have believed and have been sealed with the Holy Spirit and one of these days God, the Owner will take His possession, the Church, out of this alien order and preserve her in His presence in an order never again to be touched by evil.

This "Hymn of Salvation" pretty much summarizes the whole of the Epistle. The ideas generated in it control the rest of the book and surface again and again in a variety of ways. Thus, we have taken more pains with this majestic doxology.

A Prayer for Enlightenment
Ephesians 1:15-23

The pastoral heart of the Apostle is exposed in this section of chapter 1. His praise has turned to prayer, intercessory prayer. Phillips paraphrases verse 16, "I thank God continually for you and I never give up praying for you." These churches were under constant bombardment from nonbelieving sects and pagan religions and Paul knew they needed to be lifted to the throne of God regularly that their faith not fail under the pressures and temptations. He wanted to see growth in their spiritual lives but he also desired that they be a united people. Knowing his commitment to his churches and the spirit of prayer which pervades his letters, we must exclaim with Bruce, "What an intercessor he must have been!"[1]

The Inspiration for the Prayer

Ephesians 1:15-16

> 15 Wherefore I also, after I heard of your faith in the Lord Jesus, and love unto all the saints,
> 16 Cease not to give thanks for you, making mention of you in my prayers,

Wherefore (15) at the beginning of this section is a bridging term, at once referring back to what Paul had just declared and introducing a new line of thought. The connection runs something like this: "Because you give such clear evidence of having shared in these salvation blessings, I find myself expressing to God all the time my thanks for you and am inspired to pray for you." The gospel was bearing fruit among them. Paul has heard of their *faith in the Lord Jesus,* and *love unto all the saints* (15). Faith and love go together in the Christian life. In Galatians Paul speaks of "faith working through love" (5:6, RSV). You cannot have one without the other. A faith inspired and sustained by Christ generates love not only in the believing heart but also among the saints. Paul, hearing of this kind of life among the Ephesians, is moved to approach the throne of God in behalf of their continued spiritual maturation.

The Burden of the Prayer

Ephesians 1:17

> 17 That the God of our Lord Jesus Christ, the Father of glory, may give unto you the spirit of wisdom and revelation in the knowledge of him:

Notice the reverence of Paul in his address of God. His Jewish background had given him a profound respect for God. As a Christian his knowledge of God has expanded. God is the *God of our Lord Jesus Christ,* which is a way of saying that He is the God who enfleshed himself in Christ. He is "the High and Lifted Up One" who came near to us to share His life with us. Some years before Paul wrote this Epistle, Zechariah, the father of John the Baptist, expressed the beauty of this truth at the time of the birth of John: "Blessed be the Lord God of Israel, for he has visited [come caringly] and redeemed his people" (Luke 1:68, RSV). God had come in the Lord Jesus Christ to all mankind and Paul came to enjoy the spiritual benefits of that divine visit when he met Christ on the Damascus Road. The One who visited him in His Son is now the *Father of glory* ("all-glorious Father," NEB). The splendor of the Heavenly Father arises out of the totality of His perfections. Every good attribute originates and emanates from Him. We can come to Him in prayer with confidence knowing that He "is what He is" and "has what it takes" to respond honestly and effectively to our prayers.

The burden of the prayer is that God may give them *the spirit of wisdom and revelation in the knowledge of him.* The Greek does not have the article before *spirit,* so we are justified in deciding that Paul is praying for "a gift of wisdom and revelation," by which he means, a capacity of comprehending and applying to life all the benefits of grace through the power of its spirit. Paul is concerned that all of the experiential dimensions of what God has done for them will break in upon them so their lives will be sustained in the midst of all circumstances. They have an experiential knowledge of God, but the Apostle wants that knowledge to become keener and stronger, and be reflected in their lives in specific modes of behavior. When the Spirit of the Lord takes control of our minds as well as of our hearts, we begin to see the depths of the meaning of the revelation made in Jesus Christ. The Spirit-filled person possesses a broader insight into the things of God (see 1 Cor. 2:10-16).

Seeing with the Eyes of the Heart

Ephesians 1:18-19

> 18 The eyes of your understanding being enlightened; that ye may know what is the hope of his calling, and what the riches of the glory of his inheritance in the saints,
> 19 And what is the exceeding greatness of his power to usward who believe, according to the working of his mighty power,

One of the creative functions of the Holy Spirit is to "enlighten the inner eyes." When the spiritual eyes are healed of all astigmatism, the knowledge of God's purposes in redemption are made clearer. There are three special benefits of this enlightenment.

First, one comes to *know what is the hope of his calling,* that is, Christ's calling. "Christian hope," writes Summers, "is placed in that call."[2] The clearer vision includes an understanding of the eternal hope which salvation in Christ includes.

Second, with spiritually enlightened eyes, the Christian knows what are *the riches of the glory of his inheri-*

tance in the saints. The *saints* belong to God; they are His heritage (see v. 14; Col. 1:12). But at the same time the relationship with the Father includes an inheritance for the saints. They are heirs and joint heirs with Jesus. Opened eyes can glimpse some of the wealth of that inheritance.

Third, with spiritually enlightened eyes, the Christian comes to know *the exceeding greatness of his power* (19). In a power-conscious age, these may seem to be idle words because they relate to spiritual matters. But the operation of the power of God is not most spectacular in the natural order; rather it is demonstrated most miraculously in the spiritual realm. Nothing can match the power of God in its soul-regenerating and soul-sanctifying effects. The true greatness of God's power is seen most dramatically when His Spirit is released in the heart of a sinner and the wicked man becomes a good man, a holy man. As Summers says, "No power which man can generate or release is able to do that."[3] This power, which flows into the heart of believers, is resurrection power, the power of purity, the power of faith and hope.

Westcott points out that the three aspects of the prayer correspond with the experiences of life. He writes:

> We can face the sorrows and sadnesses of personal and social history "in the hope of God's calling." We can rejoice in the possession of capacities and needs to which our present circumstances bring no satisfaction when we look to "the wealth of the glory of God's inheritance in the saints." We can overcome the discouragements of constant failures and weaknesses by the remembrance of the power of God shown in the raising of Christ.[4]

The Supreme Manifestation of Divine Power

Ephesians 1:20-23

20 Which he wrought in Christ, when he raised him from the dead, and set him at his own right hand in the heavenly places,
21 Far above all principality, and power, and might, and dominion,

and every name that is named, not only in this world, but also in that which is to come:

22 And hath put all things under his feet, and gave him to be the head over all things to the church,

23 Which is his body, the fulness of him that filleth all in all.

In typical fashion, Paul temporarily sets aside the central concern of his prayer and literally explodes with evidential statements of the mighty power of God demonstrated in the life of Christ, His Son, in three ways.

1. *It is manifested in Christ's resurrection* (20). The measure of God's life-giving power was expressed *when he raised him* (Christ) *from the dead.* F. F. Bruce reminds us that the death of Christ is the chief demonstration of the love of God (Rom. 5:8), but the Resurrection is the chief demonstration of the power of God.[5] Paul will shortly come to say that the power that raised Jesus is "the power that worketh in us" (3:20).

2. *God's power is manifested in Christ's ascension and exaltation* (20b, 22a). Resurrection is followed by ascension into the presence of God. On the Day of Pentecost, Peter declared, "This Jesus God raised up, and of that we all are witnesses. Being therefore exalted at the right hand of God, and having received from the Father the promise of the Holy Spirit, he has poured out this which you see and hear" (Acts 2:32-33, RSV). To be seated at the right hand means that Christ has been invested with sovereignty and universal dominion (21). He is Lord over all, not so much because He is the Creator of all (Col. 1:16) but principally because He "humbled himself and became obedient unto death, even the death of the cross" (Phil. 2:8).

Saviorhood has given Him a status in the universe which no creator *in this world* or *in that which is to come* can hope to achieve (21). By His redemptive work, which has made Him the Head of the new creation, He has won this sovereignty. He not only has temporal dominion; He also has eternal dominion. His exaltation is simultaneously the subordination of all else: God has *put all things under his feet* (22). Mackay concludes that "the course of history and the destiny of the universe are both in the hands of Jesus."[6]

3. *God's power is manifested in Christ's headship of the Church* (22b-23). Christ is God's Gift to the Church. All the power vested in Christ flows into the life of the believing community. Whatever authority and power the Church has in the world, in effecting moral and spiritual change, she has by virtue of her Head, Christ. When the Church obediently and faithfully evangelizes in the name of her Lord, she possesses His rulership in the world (cf. Matt. 28:18-20; Mark 3:14 ff; John 20:21-23). The Church is *His body*—His hands, feet, mouth—indeed, His very existence now in the world. Christ has designed that His followers be Him to needy men.

The Church, as the Body of Christ, is *the fulness of him that filleth all in all* (23). This clause is the subject of much study, but apparently it means that while Christians are "being filled" by Christ to do His work in the world, the Lord himself, in some sense, is "being filled" as the Church lives as a holy people and faithfully witnesses to His grace everywhere and in every age. The Church is the receptacle of divine fullness and at the same time the completion of Christ. All the divine graces and virtues which the Church needs to be Christ in the world are available to her through her Lord who dwells in fullness in the midst of her.

The Creation of a New People

Ephesians 2:1-22

EPHESIANS 2

With chapter 2 we move from praise to God for bringing Christ from the tomb by His mighty power to a witness to that same resurrection power which miraculously raises men from spiritual death to life. *You hath he quickened, who were dead in trespasses and sins* (1). In essence Paul is saying to the Ephesians. "The same almighty hand that was laid upon the body of the dead Christ and lifted Him from Joseph's grave to the highest seat in heaven, has been laid upon your soul and has raised you from the grave and death of sin to share by faith Christ's celestial life."

The sublime nature of conversion is the theme in verses 1-10. An inextricable union exists between the miracle of Christ's resurrection and our spiritual resurrection. Findlay comments, "There is an acting over again in us of Christ's crucifixion, resurrection and ascension, when we realize through faith that which was done for mankind in Him."[1] Faith releases that power in the life and the result is that a person is raised from the death of sin unto life. We are talking about a supernatural power, this resurrection power that turns death into life. It is "the power of God unto salvation" (see Rom. 1:16). No greater day will ever dawn for the sinner than the day when God stands over his spiritually lifeless form and calls him into a whole new existence, free from the guilt and power of sin.

Throughout this second chapter a unique contrast prevails—a contrast between the old existence apart from Christ and the new existence in Christ.

Salvation by Resurrection

Ephesians 2:1-10

> 1 And you hath he quickened, who were dead in trespasses and sins;
> 2 Wherein in time past ye walked according to the course of this world, according to the prince of the power of the air, the spirit that now worketh in the children of disobedience:
> 3 Among whom also we all had our conversation in times past in the lusts of our flesh, fulfilling the desires of the flesh and of the mind; and were by nature the children of wrath, even as others.
> 4 But God, who is rich in mercy, for his great love wherewith he loved us,
> 5 Even when we were dead in sins, hath quickened us together with Christ, (by grace ye are saved;)
> 6 And hath raised us up together, and made us sit together in heavenly places in Christ Jesus:
> 7 That in the ages to come he might shew the exceeding riches of his grace in his kindness toward us through Christ Jesus.
> 8 For by grace are ye saved through faith; and that not of yourselves: it is the gift of God:
> 9 Not of works, lest any man should boast.
> 10 For we are his workmanship, created in Christ Jesus unto good works, which God hath before ordained that we should walk in them.

The contrast mentioned above is sharply depicted in the division of thought between verses 1-3 and 4-10. The first portion describes a person before faith and the second a person after faith, or the spiritual state before conversion and the spiritual state after conversion.

1. *Life before faith* (1-3). Paul distinguishes five characteristics of this life apart from God.

a. It is a life of spiritual death: *dead in trespasses and sins.* Spiritual death is "the death of sin," that is, the life of separation from God. Paul is not saying simply that the sinner is "subject to death or even under the sentence of death; he is *actually* dead, because under the control of a sinful nature."[2] The twin words, *trespasses* and *sins,* emphasize the total nature of this death. A sinner therefore is not "alive unto God" (Rom. 6:11), which is to say, God is not the source of the meaning and hope of life (see Gal. 2:19-20).

b. It is a life conducted *according to the course of this world* (2). The Greek word translated *world* literally means "age." The person apart from Christ "walks" or "leads" his or her life in conformity with the thoughts and pursuits of this present evil age (see Rom. 12:2; 1 Cor. 7:31; Gal. 1:4). For Paul, "to live a certain life is to follow a given path."[3] "Walk" here, as it does in Paul's other Epistles and the writings of John, denotes more than "an aimless promenading or strolling about." Rather, it means "a choice of steps on a given ground in a given direction." The spiritually dead person has forsaken the rules and ways of God for the rules and ways of this present order. The spirit of the age dictates the life to be lived.

c. It is also a life under the control of *the prince of the power of the air.* This world has a god, Satan. In 2 Cor. 4:4 Paul speaks of "the god of this world." In Hebrew thought, Satan was believed to exercise his authority in the world and in the upper regions short of heaven itself. He is the ruler of those "spiritual hosts of wickedness in the heavenly places" mentioned in Eph. 6:12, RSV. "Satan is an evil *spirit* which works *in the children of disobedience.*"[4] Just as Satan became possessed with a rebellious spirit, so everyone whose spiritual life is generated from his is rebellious. To speak of the sinner as being "a son of disobedience" is to suggest that the attribute of disobedience is innate to the person, not incidental. Barth reminds us that disobedience is the main sin of man. It is not nonconformity to an idea, principle, or fate, but active rejection of the Word of God.

d. It is a life submissive to the fleshly passions, *fulfilling the desires of the flesh and of the mind* (3). It is a life kept within the confines of, and controlled by, the appetites and impulses of the fallen human nature. *In the lusts of our flesh* denotes, therefore, the domain or element in which the sinful life is spent. Salmond observes that there are two sources of evil mentioned here: (1) the fallen nature of man in general, expressed in the phrase "the lusts of our flesh," and (2) "the laboratory of perverted thoughts, impressions, imaginations, volitions, in particular."[5]

Thus, the unregenerate person possesses a nature, a moral temperament disposed to evil and hostile to the leadings of the Spirit of the Lord. Furthermore, his "flesh" and "mind" relentlessly produce desires and impulses which are contrary to the will of God.

e. It is life "under the dreadful judgment of God" (NEB). The phrase *by nature the children of wrath* denotes that every person apart from the grace of God is an object of God's wrath, not only because he commits acts of sin but because he is *by nature* (innately) a sinner. There is a principle of sin in human nature, inherited from Adam, and man sins because of the operation of that principle in his life. As an unrighteous person, not having repented of his sins and believed on the Lord Jesus, man is an object of God's wrath.

A God of wrath is an offensive idea to modern man. However, throughout the Bible this truth about God is consistently taught (see Rom. 1:18; Eph. 5:6). "His wrath is a permanent and consistent element in His nature and is best seen as the reverse side of His holy love. God's wrath represents the divine hostility to all that is evil. It is a personal quality without which God would not be fully righteous."[6] God's love would easily degenerate into unsaving sentimentality if His righteousness did not cause Him to be unfailingly antagonistic to sin.

The wrath of God is a *"settled indignation,* the attitude of God toward men viewed as fallen in Adam (Rom. 5:12, 17-19) and refusing to accept the gospel of grace and salvation in Christ."[7] Jesus said that "he who does not obey the Son shall not see life, but the wrath of God rests upon him" (John 3:36, RSV). Findlay's remark on this subject says it all: "I could neither love nor fear a God who did not care enough about me to be angry with me when I sin."[8]

Notice the remarkable change in pronouns in this passage. First, Paul uses "you" in verses 1 and 2, obviously speaking of the Gentile readers. Then, in verses 3-7 he shifts to "we," intending thereby to include himself and all his Jewish friends. Even when he was characterizing the offensive behavior of others, Paul could not escape the fact that he once was in the same tragic, spiritual condition. A self-righteous Pharisee was no better than a debauched pagan.

2. *Life after faith* (4-10). These verses speak of the miracle of conversion. Notice needs to be taken of the little word "but" which is an adversative conjunction. It introduces a condition entirely opposite to what has just been described. It announces the *divine difference,* the radical change which resurrection with Christ brings about in a person's life. Thus, against the dark backdrop of the spiritual death in which the unbelieving exist, the Apostle sketches a captivating characterization of the new life that faith in Christ creates.

a. It is a God-initiated life (4-5). *But God . . . even when we were dead in sins, hath quickened us* ("made us alive," NIV, RSV) *together with Christ.* The beauty of the gospel is that the initiative to redemption is taken by God. "God was in Christ reconciling the world unto himself" (2 Cor. 5:19). The spiritually dead have neither right to, nor hope of, salvation, and yet God's love, rich (exhaustless) in mercy, is such that He desires and longs to call the dead to life. The motivation of His saving act is His love, and as Barth reminds us, *"He loves us with all his love."*

Moreover, it is neither the attractiveness of the dead nor a weakness in His own nature that moved God to come caringly to His creatures. As Deut. 7:6-9 makes plain, God showers love upon man for His own sake. "It is God's nature to love and to act out of love—'for his name's sake,' as the OT untiringly repeats."[9] Furthermore, if *all the love of God* is manifested in the resurrection of the spiritually dead, then simultaneously the heart of God is exposed to believers. Those who believe on Him and come to newness of life surely know Him for what He really is.

b. It is resurrection life (6-7). In verse 6 the word *together* appears twice. Reborn men are *raised . . . up together* with Christ and *sit together in heavenly places in Christ Jesus. Together* in this passage does not appear in the original language as a single word but as a prefix *(syn)* to the verbs *raised* and *sit*. It is a preposition of association and expresses the unique truth that our resurrection from the gloom of spiritual death, brought on by our walking in sin, is a concomitant of the resurrection of Christ. The saving power of God for all future believers was released in the moment of the raising of His Son; all the forces of evil were defeated in that massive act of rescuing Him from the tomb and death.

All who "believe in the Lord Jesus Christ" share in that victorious power and are raised into life, the domination of evil in their lives having been broken. Jesus said, "Truly, truly, I say to you, the hour is coming, and now is, when the dead will hear the voice of the Son of God, and those who hear will live" (John 5:25, RSV). "When a human soul awakes from its trespasses and sins, when the love of God is poured into a heart that was cold and empty, when the Spirit of God breathes into a spirit lying powerless and buried in the flesh, there is as true a rising from the dead as when Jesus our Lord came out from His sepulchre."[10] Such is spiritual resurrection! And all who are so raised and energized by the resurrection power of God become "one body in Christ," a fellowship of the spiritually resurrected.

Resurrection is followed by exaltation. Believers are then seated with Christ "in the heavenlies" (see 1:3). In other words, they "sit where Christ sits," enjoying a life that is above the world and directed by the will and purposes of God. The purpose of this resurrected and exalted life of the believer is *that in the ages to come he* (God)

*might show the exceeding riches of his grace in his kind-
ness toward us through Christ Jesus* (7).

c. It is a gifted life (8-10). Expanding on the parenthetical note in verse 5, Paul here presents "one of the
great evangelical summaries of the New Testament." We
might say these verses comprise "Paul's own message in a
nutshell." All that he has written in the great Epistles of
Romans and Galatians is encapsulated in these three
majestic verses. Four very important words carry the
meaning here.

(1) *Grace.* Paul begins with the statement, *By grace
are ye saved through faith* (8). "Grace," a central word
for Paul (100 instances in his writings) simply means
"unmerited favor." God has done something for us we did
not deserve or merit. Sin so possessed our lives when we
were alienated from God, we had no moral power to create
a life of righteousness that would earn us acceptance with
God. But God, working through His Son, literally gave us
our salvation. Thus, grace is a gift. Our salvation is not
the accomplishment of our good works but the free gift of
the love and mercy of God.

(2) *Saved.* The word in the Greek language can mean
"made whole," "given a satisfying life," or "rescued from
a threatening existence." In gospel terms it carries the last
definition. To be saved means to be delivered from the
power and dominion of sin. It carries the same connotation as the word "redemption" in 1:7. *Ye are saved* is
expressed in the perfect tense in the Greek, indicating an
act completed in the past but creating a condition which
continues into the present. A proper paraphrasing might
be: "You were saved at a particular moment in the past
and are now in a state or condition of salvation." There is
no "hope so" in this declaration of the Apostle. Salvation
is an accomplished fact! We see here Paul's doctrine of
assurance breaking through. Findlay observes that it was
"this confidence of present salvation that made the
Church irresistible."[11]

(3) *Faith.* Salvation comes *through faith.* Faith is the means or instrument by which God's grace unto salvation is appropriated. Faith is the free, obedient response of man to the divine offer of salvation. As one has said, "It is the hand that receives the gift."

The statement, *that not of yourselves: it is the gift of God,* has raised a troublesome question: What is the gift of God? Is it grace or faith? The little pronoun *that* produces the problem. The pronoun is neuter, but the nouns *grace* and *faith* are feminine. Thus, it could not refer to either of them. Rather it refers "to the whole preceding clause, *ye are saved through faith*" (Wesley). The Apostle has the entire process of redemption in mind. Salvation, therefore, is the gift of God. Strictly speaking, we cannot categorically assert, from this passage that faith is a gift of God. However, to the degree that God works through His Spirit to bring conviction to the sinner's heart and enlightenment to see the possibilities of a new life for himself, to that degree we can say it is a gift. The joyous heart, set free from the bondage of sin, will gladly testify, "It is all of God!"

(4) *Works.* Paul states: *We are His workmanship, created in Christ Jesus unto good works* (10). The redeemed person is a work of divine art. *Workmanship* in the original language can be used to describe a piece of literature, a sculpture, or a painting. More specifically, it refers to any finished, perfect product, a masterpiece. This work of spiritual art is *created in Christ Jesus,* by which is meant, "It takes its form and beauty from Christ." What God has determined to be the character of redemption for His fallen creatures, no man by moral effort can create. Only the divine hand can bring it into existence. And God is the Perfect Craftsman, working in and through and with the Perfect Model, Christ.

Paul never abandons the concept of good works. He says we are made new creatures that we might do *good works.* It must be kept in mind that Paul distinguishes between good works as the basis of salvation and good works as the proof of salvation. As Vaughn observes, "We are not save *by* good works, but most assuredly we are saved *for* them."[12] These works, which all the saints are enabled to perform through the power of the Spirit, constitute the fulfillment of the commandments of God which have been announced from the beginning of time. Doing these good works (see 4:11-13, 15-16) is the Church's way of carrying out her mission in the world. Personal testimony and proclamation combine to make evangelism effective.

One Body in Christ

Ephesians 2:11-22

> 11 Wherefore remember, that ye being in time past Gentiles in the flesh, who are called Uncircumcision by that which is called the Circumcision in the flesh made by hands;
> 12 That at that time ye were without Christ, being aliens from the commonwealth of Israel, and strangers from the covenants of promise, having no hope, and without God in the world:
> 13 But now in Christ Jesus ye who sometimes were far off are made nigh by the blood of Christ.
> 14 For he is our peace, who hath made both one, and hath broken down the middle wall of partition between us;
> 15 Having abolished in his flesh the enmity, even the law of commandments contained in ordinances; for to make in himself of twain one new man, so making peace;
> 16 And that he might reconcile both unto God in one body by the cross, having slain the enmity thereby:
> 17 And came and preached peace to you which were afar off, and to them that were nigh.
> 18 For through him we both have access by one Spirit unto the Father.
> 19 Now therefore ye are no more strangers and foreigners, but fellowcitizens with the saints, and of the household of God;
> 20 And are built upon the foundation of the apostles and prophets, Jesus Christ himself being the chief corner stone;
> 21 In whom all the building fitly framed together groweth unto an holy temple in the Lord:
> 22 In whom ye also are builded together for an habitation of God through the Spirit.

The first half of this chapter tells of the spiritual death from which both Jew and Gentile were resurrected and the newness of life which that resurrection power has created in them. The second half focuses on the corporate experience of believers and declares how Christ has made

Jew and Gentile into *one new man* (a single society of believers), *so making peace* (15).

1. *The Gentiles before faith* (11-12). *Wherefore remember* carries a great deal of meaning here. Paul wants the Gentiles to recall their former life of separation from the Jews and from the blessings of the covenant life. Jews and Gentiles were socially but, more important, religiously alienated from one another. Mackay speaks of "the Great Rift" which separated the two people.[13] Contemptuously, the Jews nicknamed the Gentiles the *Uncircumcision,* indicating thereby that they were really God-forsaken, spiritually illiterate people. Instead of the Jews giving all their energies to the fulfillment of their mission to the nations by sharing their knowledge of and faith in God, they segregated themselves and became spiritually proud (see Gen. 12:3; Isa. 42:1, 6; 49:6; the Book of Jonah).

Paul chastises them by calling them *the Circumcision in the flesh made by hands.* For him there is a world of difference between circumcision "in the flesh" and circumcision "of the heart." The "cutting away" of the sinful nature from the heart leaves one free to "worship God in the spirit, and rejoice in Christ Jesus, and have no confidence in the flesh" (Phil. 3:3). Be that as it may, now through the work of Christ, the chasm between the Jew and the Gentile has been bridged, and God's plan of creating a society of unity in peace is being realized.

Nevertheless, the truth about the Gentiles is that they were "spiritually bankrupt." Their spiritual assets were nil.

a. They were *without Christ* (12), which means they possessed no hope of the Messiah and thus none of the benefits that He brought to mankind. Their history was "Christless." In our day we must not forget the countless millions who have no knowledge of Christ and have no opportunity to share in the blessings of His death and resurrection.

b. They were *aliens from the commonwealth of Israel,*

which is to say, they were excluded from the rights and privileges which were accorded those in the community of faith. The people of Israel, with all their historical experiences, constitute the realm in which God's saving knowledge was revealed. Admission to that people through a faith like unto Abraham's was the way into salvation. But the Gentiles were offered no admission to this community of faith except under the most rigorous terms.

c. They were *strangers from the covenants of promise.* The Gentiles were literally nonparticipants in the privileges, present or prospective, which were pledged to Israel. God had entered into a covenant relationship with Israel—not a contract in which God and man hammered out the terms. God set the terms of the covenant because of who He is. He is the one party who can under all circumstances keep His side of any agreement. He has the resources and He does not fail. These promises were made to Abraham (Gen. 12:2-3; 15:8-21; 17:1-21), to the people of Israel, under Moses' leadership (Exod. 24:1-11), and later in the new covenant (Jer. 31:31-34). Unfortunately, the promises of God's redemptive blessings were not shared freely and consistently with the Gentiles. They were thus deprived of these potential spiritual blessings.

d. They possessed *no hope* and were *without God.* These two phrases say it all; they were spiritually desolate, bankrupt. Westcott notes the pathos of the strange combination of *without God* (literally, "atheists") and *no hope,* and comments that they faced nature and life without hope because they had no relationship with the Interpreter of nature and life. "The Gentiles had, indeed, 'gods many and lords many,' and one God as 'a first Cause' in the philosophic theories, but no God loving men and Whom men could love."[14]

2. *The Gentiles after faith* (13-18). Once again we encounter one of Paul's dramatic transitions, much like the one in verse 4. The adversative conjunction "but" is employed again, signifying the radical change of life

opposite to that which has been depicted. It speaks again of the "divine difference." The intervention of God through the life, death and resurrection of Christ has made the difference. That difference is expressed in three ways.

a. The Gentiles are brought near by the blood of Christ (13). Isaiah, centuries before, spoke the word of the Lord, announcing, "Peace, peace, to the far and to the near" (57:19, RSV). The prophet was speaking of two groups of people: "the far ones" who are the Gentiles and "the near ones" who are the Hebrews. Ephesians 2:17 reads: "So he came and proclaimed the good news: peace to you who were far off, and peace to those who were near by; for through him we both alike have access to the Father in the one Spirit" (NEB). These Gentiles, the "far ones," have been brought within range of the grace of God through *the blood of Christ,* obviously a reference to the Cross. The "whosoever" of the gospel breaks through at this point. "God so loved the world, that he gave his only begotten Son, that whosoever believeth in him should not perish, but have everlasting life" (John 3:16). The spiritually deprived need not perish in the night; they can come expectantly, yet repentantly, to the Cross where forgiveness of sin is assured. Everyone is invited.

> *There is a green hill far away,*
> *Without a city wall,*
> *Where the dear Lord was crucified,*
> *Who died to save us all.*

> —CECIL F. ALEXANDER

b. Jew and Gentile become one in Christ (14-15). The Prince of Peace (Isa. 9:6), the Source of peace, has *broken down the middle wall of partition* between the Jew and the Gentile (14). This is obviously a reference to the Temple in Jerusalem, in which a wall divided the court of the Gentiles from the court of the Jews. A Gentile dared not go beyond that wall on pain of death. This wall is, for Paul, a symbol of the division between the Jew and the Gentile. Translated into contemporary gospel terms, Paul is declaring that Christ has broken down every barrier of the spirit between men. Markus Barth has written, "To confess Jesus Christ is to affirm the abolition and end of division and hostility, the end of separation and segregation, the end of enmity and contempt, and the end of every sort of ghetto."[15] Those who are born anew by faith in Christ become one people.

More specifically in this context, the great barrier between the Jew and the Gentile was "the law of commandments and ordinances" (15, RSV). The Jewish insistence on pursuing its "kosher" way of life and rejecting all others who did not join them on those terms created serious hostilities in the ancient world. The Gentiles were repulsed by many of the Jewish rites, especially circumcision, because they themselves honored the physical body and saw this practice as a profaning of the body. Christ *in his flesh,* in His human existence and death, "nullified" or "invalidated" this whole legal system of the Jews as a way of acceptance with God, including circumcision as a sign of acceptance (see Galatians) and by so doing He removed the barrier of hostility. Foulkes observes, "The way of approach is now by grace, by a new creative work of God, the same for both Jews and Gentiles."[16]

Christ is concerned to bring into birth "a new man, a new society." This is the central purpose of His incarnation, ministry, death, resurrection, and exaltation. The first Adam, by his one act of disobedience, brought into existence a sinful, divisive race of people. But the Second Adam, by His one act of obedience to the will of God, is fathering a new humanity. This new creation is *in himself* —in vital union with Jesus Christ.

In Paul's thinking, apart from Christ, mankind is divided essentially into two races—Jews and Gentiles, but in Christ a new race comes into being—Christians. The Gentile is not turned into a Jew, nor the Jew into a Gentile. They become wholly new persons. This being the case, the

Jew no longer can be proud of his religiosity, nor can the Gentile be boastful of his worldly wisdom. The ground indeed is level at the foot of the Cross. The Prince of Peace, out of the immeasurable depths of His own tranquil spirit, died at Calvary's cross to "make peace" among us.

c. Jew and Gentile are both reconciled to God and thus are one body (16-18). Reconciliation is the key word here. It is basically Pauline (see 2 Cor. 4:18-20; Col. 1:20). In the verb form of the original Greek, "reconcile" means "to exchange completely." Used here, the idea suggests the exchange of one set of relationships for a new set. Once the Gentiles were at odds with God and with the Jews, but now they are in fellowship with God through faith in Jesus Christ. God is not the angry deity, but the Father who loves and cares for them. They are living in harmony with Him and with their fellowmen. By analogy, as angles equal to a third angle are equal to each other, so men reconciled to God are reconciled to each other. In the Body of Christ, where reconciled people worship and serve together, there is peace and together they *have access by one Spirit unto the Father* (18).

The word *access* can mean "introduction" or "entrance." *Through him,* that is, Christ, we are not only introduced to God the Father, but have ready entrance into His presence. Christ is the Way to God (John 14:6). The writer to the Hebrews exhorts us to "come boldly unto the throne of grace" (Heb. 4:16). Beare comments, "Christ brings us to know him in the fullness of his glory as the Father."[17] Because He is our Father, we know we have access to His heart and mind.

3. *The grand unity in Christ* (19-22). The deliverance of the Jewish and Gentile believers from their sins, the destruction of their hostilities toward one another, and the uniting of them into a community of trust are the results of the atoning work of Christ. Together they constitute the true Israel, the people of God. The Gentiles are *no more strangers* (foreign visitors with no rights in the com-

munity) and *foreigners* (aliens enjoying temporary and limited rights as residents).[18] They truly belong to God and their status is in no wise inferior to that of the Jews. Equality of rights prevails among all believers; there are no second-class citizens. This unity of the Church is expressed in three figures of speech.

a. A political figure: *citizens with the saints* (19b). Gentiles who were fortunate enough to hold Roman citizenship had their names engraved on a civic roll so that all persons would know their status. Likewise, now the Gentile believers have their names inscribed on the divine roster and thus possess this higher citizenship in which God is the eternal Ruler and all of His people are His willing subjects. In Christ, the "farthest out" and "nearest in" share the same privileges in the kingdom of God.

b. A familial figure: *the household of God* (19c). A Gentile who is incorporated into the new Israel finds communion with God. As a citizen of the Kingdom, he enjoys the protection of the King. But he is also a member of "God's household." He has the security of the divine family, but more than that, he is guaranteed the loving care of the Father. This "household" is the Church of Jesus Christ and exists only by the mutual support and love of all the family of believers. Moreover, family words like "brothers" and "sisters," "relatives," and "children" are appropriate for the description of what it means to be in "God's household."

c. An architectural figure: *an holy temple in the Lord* (20-22). A strange transition takes place at this point. In what follows, those who have become members of God's household are no longer described as its inhabitants, but rather are depicted as "the building materials of a house in which God himself dwells." The Gentiles, along with the believing Jews, become *an habitation of God* (22).

The Builder of the edifice is God. First Corinthians 3:9 says specifically, "Ye are God's building" (see Matt. 16:18). Certain servants of God, such as *the apostles and prophets,* constitute the *foundation* of the temple (20a). The apostles—men like Peter, James, John and Paul—laid the basis for the Church by their faithful proclamation of the Word of Christ. Prophets, along with inspired teachers and preachers, added to the strength of the foundation. Wesley observes that "the word of God, declared by the apostles and prophets, sustains the faith of all believers."[19] The unique relationship of the preacher to the proclamation of the Word allows us, therefore, to speak of the preacher as the foundation.

Christ is *the chief corner stone* of the building (20b). "The stone which the builders rejected has become the head of the corner," the Psalmist declares (118:22, RSV). This figure seems to suggest that Christ not only controls the shape and form of the Church, but is also her identification. If Christ is not present in her life, the Church does not belong to Him.

Believers in Christ are the building stones of the ever-growing temple of God. In this figure Paul may be thinking of a complex of buildings under construction. On the other hand, he may have in mind the idea that this single temple is still being built. Accepting this latter interpretation, Mackay writes: "New living stones must continue to be added to the incompleted building, and those there already, and those still to be laid in the sacred structure, must 'grow into an holy temple in the Lord.'"[20] By reference to growth, Paul must have in mind the need of God's people to take responsibility for her spiritual life, be aggressive in her evangelism, and be decisive in her stand against destructive activities (Eph. 4:16; see 1 Cor. 3:6-7). The agency of this growth, that is the One who enables the Church to increase, is *the Spirit* (22). "The Holy Spirit is the Supreme Builder of the Church, as He is the supreme witness to Jesus Christ (John 15:26, 27)."[21]

A Prayer for Divine Fullness

Ephesians 3:1-21

EPHESIANS 3

Paul's Stewardship of the Mystery

Ephesians 3:1-13

1 For this cause I Paul, the prisoner of Jesus Christ for you Gentiles,

2 If ye have heard of the dispensation of the grace of God which is given me to you-ward:

3 How that by revelation he made known unto me the mystery; (as I wrote afore in few words,

4 Whereby, when ye read, ye may understand my knowledge in the mystery of Christ)

5 Which in other ages was not made known unto the sons of men, as it is now revealed unto his holy apostles and prophets by the Spirit;

6 That the Gentiles should be fellowheirs, and of the same body, and partakers of his promise in Christ by the gospel:

7 Whereof I was made a minister, according to the gift of the grace of God given unto me by the effectual working of his power.

8 Unto me, who am less than the least of all saints, is this grace given, that I should preach among the Gentiles the unsearchable riches of Christ;

9 And to make all men see what is the fellowship of the mystery, which from the beginning of the world hath been hid in God, who created all things by Jesus Christ:

10 To the intent that now unto the principalities and powers in heavenly places might be known by the church the manifold wisdom of God,

11 According to the eternal purpose which he purposed in Christ Jesus our Lord:

12 In whom we have boldness and access with confidence by the faith of him.

13 Wherefore I desire that ye faint not at my tribulations for you, which is your glory.

Having boldly declared in chapter 2 his thesis that God's eternal purpose is to unite Jews and Gentiles in "one new man" in Christ Jesus, Paul now turns again to prayer for his readers. His request climaxes in the enchanting clause in verse 19: *that ye might be filled with all the fulness of God.* The phrase *for this cause* (1,14) refers back to the previous section of the Epistle with its eloquent message that Christ by His death "demolished the Jew-Gentile and God-man barriers, and is now creating in relation to himself a single, multi-cultural human society, which is both the family God loves and the temple he lives in."[1] This is the basis of the urge to pray. In effect Paul is saying, "With this in mind I make my prayer." Griffith comments,

> You really ought to have something in mind before you make a prayer. You can't pray out of a mental vacuum or you won't know what to pray for and you won't know whom you are praying *to.* In order to talk intelligently to God you have to pray out of a mind well-furnished with ideas about God—what God is like, what he has done, what he is doing, what he can be expected to do.[2]

It is noteworthy that Paul immediately digresses and does not make his prayer until verse 14 where the words, *for this cause,* appear again. Verses 2-13 comprise a long parenthesis of very great importance, because it states again *the mystery of the gospel* and Paul's mission in the world as it relates to the mystery. This section divides itself into two parts: (1) The revelation of the mystery, and (2) The ministry of the mystery.

1. *The revelation of the mystery* (1-6). In 1:1 Paul calls himself "an apostle of Jesus Christ"; here he speaks of himself as *the prisoner of Jesus Christ* (see 4:1; 2 Tim. 1:8; Philem. 9). While this phrase undoubtedly refers to his imprisonment in Rome, it carries with it a deeper meaning. Like the term "slave," which Paul uses so frequently, *prisoner* denotes that he is bound to Christ, shut up to the life into which Christ, his Lord, has thrust him for the benefit of the Gentiles. Languishing in prison was only the external dimension of his commitment to doing

the will of his Lord. Barth observes that Paul's self-description expresses a "combination of external and internal captivity."[3]

a. Paul's special stewardship (2). The Apostle reminds them *of the dispensation of the grace of God* which was given to him in their behalf. The word *dispensation* denotes an arrangement or plan. It suggests the modes in which Paul had been selected for this special ministry. It was not of his own choosing but was a divine arrangement or plan by which the grace of God was given to him for their beneift. The NEB translates this verse as follows: "Surely you have heard how God has assigned the gift of his grace to me for your benefit." God had given to him the stewardship of dispensing the grace to the Gentiles. This concept of responsibility in service to others is not unlike that which the 12 apostles were given. Jesus said to them that "He who receives you receive me" (Matt. 10:40, NIV, RSV). Paul's ministry did not arise out of a human compulsion to share, but rather was the outworking of the grace of God in his heart. Personal enjoyment of God's saving grace and ministry flow out of the same fountain.

b. The mystery of Christ (3-6). "Revelation" is an important word for Paul. His knowledge of God and of His saving grace toward the Gentiles came not by clever reasoning on his part but by a special disclosure of God to him. This new understanding was not his alone; it has been given also by the Holy Spirit to the *holy apostles and prophets* (5). This revelation concerns *the mystery of Christ* (4). Paul had mentioned it earlier (1:9), but now he spells it out in specific details as it relates to his readers.

"Mystery" was a special word among the Gentiles, especially among those who were members of the mystery cults which flourished in that day. These mystery religions reserved their esoteric secrets for only their members who, as a result, came to think of themselves as the spiritually elite. Not so with the Christian religion. The "deep things of God" (1 Cor. 2:10) were made available to all persons in the coming of Christ. Christ himself, being the Truth, opened up all the "mysteries" of God. So, for Paul, mystery did not denote something dark, obscure, secret, and puzzling, but the "open secret" of God's saving act in Christ. What was heretofore hidden from human knowledge or understanding has now been disclosed by God through Jesus Christ.

This mystery is *the mystery of Christ,* by which is meant that He, Christ, is the source and substance of it. When we come to Christ in faith we gain insight not only into the nature of God, but also into His eternal plan to redeem everyone, both Jew and Gentile, meaning thereby all mankind.

The precise nature of that *mystery of Christ* is *that the Gentiles should be fellowheirs, and of the same body, and partakers of his promise in Christ* (6), that is, the divine promise of salvation through Christ. Paul's commitment to the unity of the body of believers breaks through here in unmistakable clarity. He uses three terms, each of which has the prefix *syn,* "together with," and shows how the Gentile Christians are one with the Jewish believers. Gentiles are "coheirs" *(synklēronoma),* "concorporate" *(syssōma),* and "cosharers" *(symmetocha)* of the promise which was given to the sons of Abraham. "What Paul is declaring is that the Gentile and Jewish Christian together are now fellow heirs of the same blessings, fellow-members of the same body and fellow-partakers of the same promise."[4]

The apostle says that the mystery *in other ages was not made known unto the sons of men,* but *is now revealed unto his holy apostles and prophets by the Spirit* (5; see Col. 1:26). The salvation of the Gentiles is certainly indicated in the Old Testament (Gen. 12:3; Isa. 49:6), but this statement by Paul is intended to stress the unveiling of the truth that Gentiles can and should be intimately joined with Jews in one body. The destruction of the centuries-old barriers between the races can and will be accomplished. Stott concludes that "the theocracy (the

Jewish nation under God's rule) would be terminated, and replaced by a new international community, the church; that this church would be 'the body of Christ', organically united to him; and that the Jews and Gentiles would be incorporated into Christ and his church on equal terms without any distinction."[5] All of this comes *by the gospel,* which announces the mystery as now an "open secret" so that people can come to hear it, believe it, and experience it.

2. *The ministry of the mystery* (7-13). Paul's deep sense of mission surfaces repeatedly as he reflects on what God has done and is doing among the Gentiles. His ministry is a service to the mystery, this bringing together of Jew and Gentile into one trusting and holy people. Five illuminating aspects of his ministry find expression in this section.

a. He was called by God (7). His role as a minister (*diakonos,* servant) was not self-chosen, for he says he *was made a minister.* This privilege of serving the Gentiles was gifted by God; it was *according to the gift of the grace of God.* The sovereign God, in unmerited action, laid his hand upon the persecutor from Tarsus and sent him to the Gentiles. Furthermore, this ambassadorial responsibility for the Gentiles came by *the effectual working* of the divine power. *Effectual working* translates a Greek word from which we get our word "energy." Paul is saying he was equipped for the task by "the energizing of the divine power." An effective, redemptive ministry originates with God as He dispenses this "saving energy" through us as His servants.

b. He considers this ministry as "an enormous privilege" (8). In spite of the fact that he was "less than the least of all Christians" (Phillips), this unexpected gift of ministry was given to him. Once he blasphemed and persecuted and insulted Christ; now he holds apostolic authority. Someone has observed that while he was "minimizing himself he magnified his office."

c. His ministry has a twofold thrust: first, to *preach*

among the Gentiles the unsearchable riches of Christ; second, *to make all men see what is the fellowship of the mystery* (8-9). The *riches of Christ* include the compassion, forgiveness, sanctification, and sustaining power of God which Christ has made available to all needy persons. To say that they are *unsearchable* is to say that they are "trackless, inexplorable, not in the sense that any part is inaccessible, but that the whole is too vast to be mapped out and measured."[6]

> *Oh, the unsearchable riches of Christ,*
> *Wealth that can never be told!*
> *Riches exhaustless of mercy and grace,*
> *Precious, more precious than gold!*

> —Fanny J. Crosby

The first responsibility of the Apostle is to evangelize the Gentiles, but at the same time he must seek to enlighten all mankind as to how the revealed truth meets the needs of all. Ministry is not only "the announcing of good news" (evangelizing), it is also the illuminating of the darkened minds of men. Paul understood his commission as that of opening the eyes of the Gentiles, "that they may turn from darkness to light and from the power of Satan to God" (Acts 26:18, RSV). The plan of the mystery, which reaches beyond the beginning of time, is that through the reconciling grace of God a whole new order of men will come into being. Faithful evangelization and teaching of the Word hold promise of just that kind of result.

d. Through the church, Paul's ministry leads to "the display of God's wisdom before the intelligences of the heavenly order"[7] (10-12). *To the intent* means "in order that" and suggests that as the Church, composed of Jews and Gentiles in unity, is brought into being, the angelic hosts come to understand *the manifold wisdom of God.* These heavenly beings also have an interest in the fulfillment of the divine plan of redemption (see 1 Pet. 1:12). The apostles and prophets have received the truth regarding God's purposes and have communicated it to the Church. The Church, in turn, mediated the truth to the whole universe.

When the Church fulfills her mission in the world, not only will the powerful rulers of the heavens see the manifold (variegated, multicolored) wisdom of God, but Paul's ministry will be validated. We all have a stake in God's redemptive scheme. His plan perfectly conforms to His holy nature and it leads only to the best for all who share in its fulfillment. But this result depends upon the divine control and use of our collective capacities as His redeemed community.

Stott comments,

> The major lesson taught by this first half of Ephesians is the biblical centrality of the church. Some people construct a Christianity which consists entirely of a personal relationship to Jesus Christ and has virtually nothing to do with the church. Others make a grudging concession to the need for church membership, but add that they have given up the ecclesiastical institution as hopeless. . . . We can safely say that God has not abandoned his church, however displeased with it he may be. . . . And if God has not abandoned it, how can we? It has a central place in his plan.[8]

All that God is about is in keeping with His "eternal purpose which he accomplished in Christ Jesus our Lord" (11, NIV). *Confidence* (12) should characterize our ministry because Christ has provided us with *boldness* and *access* to the Father. *Boldness* and *access* might well be translated a "freedom of address" and "freedom of approach." *By the faith of him*—not Christ's faith, but our faith in Him—we can approach God directly and freely and ask for every resource necessary for ministry as His people.

e. The sufferings which his ministry has brought to Paul's life have brought glory to his readers (13). At that very time Paul was chained 24 hours a day to a Roman soldier. Perhaps he thought his readers were doubting the truth of the gospel, and were saying, "If his gospel were true and he were doing the Lord's work, he would not be in prison." Paul's theory of the Cross and its meaning for the true disciple lies behind the statement that his tribulations were their *glory*. In Col. 1:24 he wrote, "I now rejoice in my sufferings for you, and fill up that which is behind of the afflictions of Christ in my flesh for his body's sake, which is the church."

Christ was glorified (His true nature revealed) in the giving of His life at Calvary. So, Paul believed the glory of his own ministry was to be found in sharing the sufferings of his Lord, in the taking up his cross daily and following Christ. The conversion of his readers, in Paul's understanding, was the glory of his ministry. As he shared in their new lives through his ministry, they, in turn, shared in his ministry. His sufferings, therefore, authenticated their experiences because they at the same time authenticated his ministry. What is his glory is theirs too. So he implores them to take heart.

The Petition for Divine Fullness

Ephesians 3:14-21

> 14 For this cause I bow my knees unto the Father of our Lord Jesus Christ,
> 15 Of whom the whole family in heaven and earth is named.
> 16 That he would grant you, according to the riches of his glory, to be strengthened with might by his Spirit in the inner man;
> 17 That Christ may dwell in your hearts by faith; that ye, being rooted and grounded in love,
> 18 May be able to comprehend with all saints what is the breadth, and length, and depth, and height;
> 19 And to know the love of Christ, which passeth knowledge, that ye might be filled with all the fullness of God.
> 20 Now unto him that is able to do exceeding abundantly above all that we ask or think, according to the power that worketh in us,
> 21 Unto him be glory in the church by Christ Jesus throughout all ages, world without end. Amen.

At this point Paul returns to prayer. Notice the phrase *for this cause* which was originally written at verse 1. What is the *cause?* The extension of mercy and grace to the Gentiles and the simultaneous bringing of them into the believing community with all the Jews who also believe in Christ! Recalling his readers' enjoyment of the reconciliation of the Cross, the peace of a covenant relationship with God, and their incorporation into the household of God, and thinking of their need to mature in the faith, Paul prays that those new Christians may come to experience the new life in Christ to its fullest. Apart from the prayers of our Lord, the New Testament records no prayer more sublime in passion and intercession than this one. Bishop Handley Moule asks: "Who has not read and re-read the closing verses of the third chapter of the Ephesians with the feeling of one permitted to look through parted curtains into the Holiest Place of the Christian life?"[9]

1. *The address of the prayer* (14-15). The intensity and urgency of the prayer of this apostle with the pastoral heart are seen in the fact that he says, *I bow my knees.* Customarily, the Jews stood to pray, usually with arms outstretched to heaven (see Matt. 6:5; Luke 18:11, 13). In a posture of deep burden and prostration before his God, Paul makes his earnest petition that God would make the youthful church "what the church can never make itself" but what it must become if it is to be what God desires it to be in the world. It must be a medium of grace to lost mankind. Posture is not to be construed as the indicator of true prayer, but it is the experience of countless Christians that sometimes the bending of the knee seems the only appropriate way to pray.

It is *unto the Father of our Lord Jesus Christ* that Paul prays. Through adoption we gain a sense of belonging to God and with that comes a realization that He is our Father and we can call Him "Abba, Father" (see Rom. 8:14-17; Gal. 4:6). As Father, God will not trifle with us when we make our petitions; He will, in His time, answer our prayers. Fatherhood gets its meaning from His fathering of His children. All our concepts of family love, including a faithful father, originate in God. Moreover, *the whole family* (15) of believers, Jews and Gentiles alike, is a creation of the Heavenly Father. The family *in heaven and earth* may well refer to the Church Militant on earth and the Church Triumphant in heaven, which together, though separated by death, are nevertheless the one great family of God.

Two important truths about prayer break through here. First, instruction, Bible reading, witnessing, teaching, and a host of other Christian activities are vitally important to maturation, but prayer is absolutely essential. Prayer for ourselves and prayer for others should have top priority in the Christian life. Second, when we make our way to the place of prayer, we must remember, as Lloyd-Jones exhorts, that "the Name that is on us is the Name of God, 'from whom the whole family in heaven and earth is named.' The family name which I claim is the Name of God, and I am to live in this world as one who represents that family, as one who represents that Father."[10] It is His name and to Him that we make our prayers.

2. *The content of the prayer* (16-19). The grammatical construction of this section makes it difficult to determine the precise focus of the prayer. It has been suggested that the axis is found in the last clause, *that ye might be filled with all the fulness of God* (19). All the other expressions are to be considered phases of this fullness. On the other hand, given the reference to the Trinity, this last expression may simply be Paul's way of relating the meaning of this experience to God the Father. Thus, to be strengthened by the Spirit, to have Christ dwelling permanently within, and to be filled with all the fullness of God are one and the same experience.

Some persons may be puzzled by the nature of this prayer, in that it very definitely calls for a radically new experience with God. Are these readers not Christians? Surely they are, for Paul calls them "saints" (1:1) and he witnesses to their having trusted the word, the gospel of salvation (1:13). Obviously, the Apostle is praying that they may enter into a deeper relationship with God. As Lloyd-Jones observes, "The Apostle is not writing a circular letter to apostles, he is not concerned here only with some very exceptional persons; he is writing to the ordinary church members of the Church of Ephesus. . . . He prays that they may experience all these blessings, leading to the almost incredible climax, 'that ye may be filled with all the fulness of God'."[11]

For Wesleyans, born-again Christians are called to enter by faith into this richer relationship with God because of the need to experience deliverance from the Adamic sin in the heart. Each phase of the prayer of Paul is couched in terms in the original Greek which indicate action that can be initiated and completed at a point in time. So Paul is petitioning for that which can be experienced here and now, in the ongoing events of one's life, so the believer can be a victorious Christian.

a. Strengthened with might by his Spirit in the inner man (16). Paul is speaking of that second experience of the Christian in which "the Holy Spirit of Promise, the Lord of Pentecost, the Spirit of Counsel and Might" invades the heart in fullness and cleansing, and reinforcing it with divine love. His petition is that they may be "fortified, braced, invigorated," and may be grasped more firmly by the Spirit. The prayer therefore is that the Holy Spirit may touch "the master spring of the whole life," controlling, strengthening, and vitalizing it for life and for service to God.

b. Christ dwelling in the heart *by faith* (17). Concurrently with the strengthening of the Spirit is the indwelling of Christ. This is another way of defining the nature of this new experience. The word for "dwell" in the Greek is derived from a word meaning "to settle down," "to take up permanent residence." Christ comes therefore "not as a Guest, precariously detained, but as a Master resident in His proper home."[12] The passionate spirit of the Apostle longs for the constant victory of his children in the faith. So he prays to the Father that

Christ will be allowed to settle down in their hearts as a permanent resident, as Lord to reign, and as Creator of the holy life of love within.

c. Rooted and grounded in love (17b). The Spirit-strengthened and Christ-indwelt life will be *rooted and grounded* in *agape,* this special quality of personhood most characteristic of God. These Christians are to have "deep roots and firm foundations" (NEB). Using these two metaphors, botanical and architectural respectively, Paul likens the results of this experience to a well-rooted tree and a well-built house. Both *rooted* and *grounded* are participles in the Greek and suggest completed action, the effects of which continue throughout the life. Paul therefore is praying for a dynamic relationship with God *in love,* the essence of this Spirit-created life. Love is "the *soil* in which the life is rooted" and "the *character* of its foundations." Perfect love in the heart makes for growth and stability (see 1 John 4:12, 17). Dale summarizes, "Love will not be an intermittent impulse, or even a constant force struggling for its rightful supremacy over baser passions; its authority will be secure; it will be the law of their whole nature; it will be the very life of their life."[13]

When Christ, who in himself is the essence of love, takes permanent residence in the heart, the Christian begins to *comprehend with all saints,* that is, to "lay hold of," "to grasp," along with all those in the community of believers, the expansive nature of *agape.* The dimension of that love is dramatically expressed in the four words *breadth, length, depth,* and *height* (18). Summers concludes that this is "another instance of Paul's piling up words for the sake of dramatic expression," but "it is a tribute to all-encompassing love of Christ."[14] Stott, on the other hand, feels it is legitimate to say that "the love of Christ is 'broad' enough to encompass all mankind (especially Jews and Gentiles, the theme of these chapters), 'long' enough to last for eternity, 'deep' enough to reach the most degraded sinner and 'high' enough to exalt him to heaven."[15]

This love of Christ for us, that brought the Son from the throne of heaven to live among us and to die for us, is beyond our finite minds to comprehend yet we can have experiential knowledge of it. We can sense in a measure its mercy, forgiveness, and purifying qualities. As Hodge concludes, "We may know how excellent, how wonderful, how free, how disinterested, how long-suffering, it is, and that is infinite."[16] He goes on to say that this is the highest and most sanctifying knowledge.

d. *Filled with all the fulness of God* (19b). Moving from the references to the Spirit and the Son, Paul now speaks of this new relationship for the believer as it relates to God. On the basis of faith, the Christian can be "filled with the godlike fullness." Fullness here is not to be taken as that which makes God infinite but rather "the fullness of grace" originating in and defined by God's own nature. Adam Clarke understands the fullness of God to be all the gifts and graces which He has promised to bestow on man in order to effect his salvation. "To be filled with all the fulness of God is to have the heart emptied of and cleansed from all sin and defilement and filled with humility, meekness, gentleness, goodness, justice, holiness, mercy, and truth and love to God and man."[17] Clarke further observes that the person *filled with all the fulness of God* has a "constant, pious, affectionate obedience" to God and "an unvarying benevolence" toward his neighbor. Such a man, he says, is saved *from* all *sin.* The tense of the verb *filled* denotes, according to Martin, that "this experience is not looked upon as something gradually acquired, but is thought of as some positive experience of the believer."[18]

3. *The doxology* (20-21). Concluding his prayer, Paul breaks out into a doxology, a magnificent declaration of the possibility of knowing this kind of relationship with God. He has no doubts that "what God promises He

performs; what He commands He enables." Three truths in a majestic crescendo of confidence come to expression here. First, God is able to do all things. Second, the scope of God's ability exceeds all the hopes and imaginings of the human heart. Third, a relationship exists between the believer's present enjoyment of divine power in conversion and the infinite ability of God to do that for which the Apostle has just prayed, that is, that they be Spirit-strengthened, Christ-indwelt, and God-filled. And the glory must all belong to Him whose love is beyond our comprehension and whose power can only be stymied by our lack of faith.

The Unity of the Church

Ephesians 4:1-16

EPHESIANS 4

In the three chapters just finished, the apostle Paul has concentrated on the theme of redemption for all men, Jew and Gentile alike, through Jesus Christ. The far reaches of that plan of redemption include the uniting of all things, in heaven and earth, in Christ. This is the eternal and gracious purpose of God which is being steadily worked out in history. A new society of men has come into existence as a result of the incarnation, death, and resurrection of Christ, the supreme expression of the love of God. Jew and Gentile are now being brought together into a new race of persons known as Christians; in fact, all the barriers separating men from God and from one another have been provisionally broken down, so this new community of love can be formed in Christ, the Prince of Peace, thus bringing peace.

Through the next three chapters the Apostle will discuss the ethical standards which must guide the new people of God. He will attempt to show what this relationship to God means for day-by-day living, whether in personal or group relationships. He turns from what God has done to what we must be and do; in other words, from doctrine to duty, from exposition to exhortation, or, as one has expressed it, "from mind-stretching theology to its down-to-earth, concrete implications in everyday living."

The Call to Unity

Ephesians 4:1-6

> 1 I therefore, the prisoner of the Lord, beseech you that ye walk worthy of the vocation wherewith ye are called,
> 2 With all lowliness and meekness, with longsuffering, forbearing one another in love;
> 3 Endeavouring to keep the unity of the Spirit in the bond of peace.
> 4 There is one body, and one Spirit, even as ye are called in one hope of your calling;
> 5 One Lord, one faith, one baptism,
> 6 One God and Father of all, who is above all, and through all, and in you all.

God's answer to the disharmony of the world is Christ. All men become one, no barriers separating them, as they live in Christ. These united believers constitute the Church, and their corporate mission is to "be Christ" in the world. They are to be witnesses to Christ's power to bring all mankind into oneness, and to faithfully live out that oneness before the world. Barth observes: "The Church has its place and function between Christ and the world. She is not the mediator of salvation; she is not the saviour of the world; she is not even a redemptive community. But she knows and makes known the Saviour and salvation."[1] As she lives worthily before the world, the Church indeed ministers Christ to others. Unity therefore is prime evidence that she belongs not to the world with its evil forces but to God.

1. *The worthy walk* (1). The prisoner Paul exhorts: *Walk worthy of the vocation wherewith ye are called.* He pleads with them to conduct their lives in keeping with the nature of their calling. He is not using the idea of "calling" to refer to special ministries in the church. Rather, he means to speak of the salvation call to which all Christians have responded by virtue of their having come to Christ. Conversion, in one sense, is a call from sin (Matt. 11:28-30) but in another sense it is a call to live a certain kind of life. Our vocation as Christians is to live out, through the power of the Spirit, the benefits of saving grace. We must conduct our lives in a manner as to show that we have been "raised from spiritual death unto life."

2. *The four graces of unity* (2). The worthy walk evidences itself in at least four graces or virtues. *Lowliness* is the opposite of pride. It is "a thankful sense of dependence upon" and a "humble recognition of the worth and value of other people." *Meekness* is more than modesty and recognition of one's limitations. Hodge says it is that "unresisting, uncomplaining disposition of mind, which enables one to bear without irritation or resentment the faults and injuries of others."[2] *Longsuffering* is "the enduring, unweariable spirit," which is able to outlast pain or provocation because of a close relationship to the long-suffering Christ. This virtue has a strong note of hope in it; it looks expectantly for improvement in fragmented situations or fractured relationships. *Forbearing . . . in love* is a twin of long-suffering and suggests a patience which goes on loving and respecting others despite their faults and weaknesses. It carries also the expectation of change as the Spirit continues to work in their hearts.

Paul's concern here is with the spiritual integrity of the Christian community, the Church. Inevitably, conflicts and tensions develop in the life of the church, but an inescapable responsibility rests upon every believer to practice these virtues of unity in order to avoid disruptive conflicts and to resolve them immediately whenever they arise.

3. *A unity-keeping responsibility* (3). Paul brings to sharp focus his emphasis on "a worthy walk," exemplified in the four graces of unity, by reminding his readers that they have an obligation to maintain the unity: *endeavouring to keep the unity of the Spirit.* The word *endeavouring* is an intensive word in the Greek, meaning, "sparing no effort." Openness to the ministry of the Spirit is the way by which this responsibility can be fulfilled, for it is the gift of the Holy Spirit which unifies the individual heart and also blends in love the body of believers. The Holy Spirit is both the originating and sustaining cause of unity. Living with a sensitive attitude toward the Spirit's guidance will guarantee a harmonious and peaceful people. The word *bond* is descriptive of a chain, and Paul is saying that the Holy Spirit uses peace as a chain to bind together all the believers and to make them one. Peaceful relationships with God and with one another make for a united church. Phillips paraphrases this verse as follows: "Make it your aim to be at one in the Spirit, and you will be bound together in peace."

4. *The basis of unity* (4-6). Oneness triggers in Paul's mind the truth that every aspect of the Christian religion declares and, when understood, evokes unity. Oneness is, therefore, "the name of the game." Mackay speaks of Paul's "seven great unities" which fall into three groups. First, there is *one body,* and *one Spirit,* [and] *one hope.* The connection between these three is as follows: "The *one body* is vitalized by the *one Spirit* and moves progressively towards the *one hope.*" The second group is composed of *one Lord, one faith, one baptism.* "Loyalty to the *one Lord* gives birth to the *one faith* and is signalized by the one act of *baptism.*"[3]

Every other unity exists and is sustained because of the oneness of the Godhead. There is *one God and Father of all, who is above all, and through all, and in you all*

(6). These descriptive phrases have special meaning for Paul, too, as Summers points out: "This one God is 'over all' in the sense of his transcendence or sovereignty; he is 'through all' in the sense of his pervading presence or immanence; he is 'in all' in the sense of his constant indwelling presence through the Holy Spirit given to all believers."[4]

One baptism has evoked considerable discussion. Some interpreters see it as a reference to water baptism, since it is a sign of initiation into the *one body,* the Church (1 Cor. 12:13). Others see it as a reference to Spirit baptism, relating it specifically to the coming of the Holy Spirit on the Day of Pentecost. This baptism is Christ's special baptism, namely, the outpouring of the Holy Spirit on the infant Church (see Matt. 3:11; Acts 1:5; 2:33). Christ's baptism comes as evidence of the new dispensation of the Spirit.

Still others in the Wesleyan tradition interpret the *one baptism* as the baptism with the Holy Spirit, a second definite work of grace. The central argument in support of this view is the fact that the Apostle does not refer to so important a rite as the Lord's Supper. Thus, when speaking of baptism, he does not have the rite of water baptism in mind but rather this special work of the Spirit in the hearts of the Christians. John 17:19 with its strong emphasis on the unifying work of sanctification wrought by the baptism with the Holy Spirit also lends support to this view.

Diversity in Unity

Ephesians 4:7-16

> 7 But unto every one of us is given grace according to the measure of the gift of Christ.
> 8 Wherefore he saith, When he ascended up on high, he led captivity captive, and gave gifts unto men.
> 9 (Now that he ascended, what is it but that he also descended first into the lower parts of the earth?
> 10 He that descended is the same also that ascended up far above all heavens, that he might fill all things.)

11 And he gave some, apostles; and some, prophets; and some, evangelists; and some, pastors and teachers;

12 For the perfecting of the saints, for the work of the ministry, for the edifying of the body of Christ;

13 Till we all come in the unity of the faith, and of the knowledge of the Son of God, unto a perfect man, unto the measure of the stature of the fulness of Christ:

14 That we henceforth be no more children, tossed to and fro, and carried about with every wind of doctrine, by the sleight of men, and cunning craftiness, whereby they lie in wait to deceive;

15 But speaking the truth in love, may grow up into him in all things, which is the head, even Christ:

16 From whom the whole body fitly joined together and compacted by that which every joint supplieth, according to the effectual working in the measure of every part, maketh increase of the body unto the edifying of itself in love.

To this point Paul has been majoring on the unity of the whole body of believers, but now he recognizes that the *one body* is made up of many members, who enjoy diverse endowments by the Spirit and who function in multiple ways in the life of the Church. The divine distribution of spiritual gifts is the source of some of the diversity in the church. Paul has already dealt with this problem in his correspondence with the Corinthians, to whom he wrote that "men have different gifts, but it is the same Spirit who gives them" (1 Cor. 12:4, Phillips).

1. *The law of the bestowal of these gifts* is that each *is given grace according to the measure of the gift of Christ* (7; see also Rom. 12:6). *Grace* in this instance does not refer to saving grace but rather to the special endowment for ministry given to Christians (see 3:7). The law which governs the granting of gifts is not only the variation in human abilities, but the pleasure and will of the sovereign God (see 1 Cor. 12:11). "Each gets the grace which Christ has to give, and each gets it in the proportion in which the Giver is pleased to bestow it; one having it in larger measure and another in smaller, but each getting it from the same hand and with the same purpose."[5] All the gift-giving relates finally to our relationship to Christ and is the outflow of the favor extended to us by the Father in Jesus Christ, who is himself the great, divine Gift. Each

person receives a gift, or gifts, as part of, and in proportion to, the grace he has received in Christ.

2. *The source of the gifts is the ascended Lord* (8-10). Employing as a lead Ps. 68:18 (which speaks of the Lord returning triumphantly to his sanctuary after defeating Israel's enemies and distributing the booty to his people), Paul depicts Christ, following His death and resurrection, ascending to heaven as a conqueror laden with spoils and leading a line of captives with Him. In that act He distributes gifts to men for their efficient and effective functioning in His church. The ascended, exalted Christ, who fills the universe with His presence and who rules the Church, is the One who endows His people for His ministry (9-10). One should not be disturbed that Paul speaks of Christ as the Giver of the gifts, whereas in other places he assigns this task either to the Spirit or to God. In his mind the persons of the Trinity are not to be separated. "Together they are involved in every aspect of the church's well being."[6]

3. *The gifts of Christ are really functions of ministry* (11). They are bestowed for the expansion and nurture of the church. The *one gift* of Christ himself unfolds in *diverse ministries*. The *apostles* are the chief ministers, Christ's special delegates who go abroad preaching, having received special instruction from the Lord. The *prophets* are those persons whose ministries possess a special insight into the present and future work of God. The *evangelists* are the itinerants who take the Word into new regions and who give special attention to the winning of unbelievers. The *pastors* are shepherds of a flock of communicants. They feed the flock and protect them from hidden spiritual dangers. They also have the function of teaching.

All of these ministries are Spirit-inspired and are the special gift of Christ. Barth points out a unique element in this listing. "All of the ministers listed are persons who fulfill their service by speaking: they are 'Ministers of the Word.'"[7] We are not to assume that Paul was playing down the other ministries in the Church as listed in 1 Cor. 12:28-30, but rather that he was emphasizing the centrality of the Word in the ministry of the Church.

4. *The purpose of the gifts is fourfold in nature* (12-16).

a. These ministries are given to edify or build up *the body of Christ* (12). *The perfecting of the saints* more properly means "the equipping of the saints" for the work of the ministry. The entire community, lay and clergy together, has been called to ministry, and the special gifts are to the end of outreach. The grand and reciprocal result of faithful use of the gifts is the building up of the Body of Christ. Growth comes by an active, passionate, and intelligent ministry on the part of the whole body of believers.

b. These gifts of ministry are given to foster maturation in the life of the Church (13). Paul uses three phrases, each one introduced by the Greek preposition *eis,* meaning "into" or "to": (1) *in the unity of the faith;* (2) *unto a perfect man;* (3) *unto the measure of the stature of the fulness of Christ.* These are not parallel ideas. The first one speaks of the *means* of maturity, the second the *reality* of maturity, and the third the *measure* of maturity. Unity in commitment to, and intimacy with Christ is the means of maturity. The reality of maturity is a life of completeness in holiness and righteousness which God enables His people to enjoy. The measure of that maturity is *the fulness of Christ,* that is, "the sum of qualities which make Him what He is."[8] Paul is speaking here of the maturation of the corporate body. As the Church matures, individual Christians mature, and vice versa.

c. These gifts of ministry are given to insure stability in the church in the face of divergent doctrines and the deceitful practices of men (14). This is a corollary of the previous statement. One of the clear evidences of immaturity of lack of growth is the inability to withstand intelligently and spiritually the claims of false doctrines. *Tossed to and fro* and *carried about* are highly dramatic terms. Immature Christians are like boats tossing uncontrollably on the waves and swinging about violently in a storm. The task of ministers is to lay a heavy hand on the rudder of the Church, to hold it steady, and to provide doctrinal ballast through a faithful preaching and teaching ministry.

d. These gifts of ministry are given to make possible a growth into Christ in every respect (15-16). The central phrase here is *in all things,* or "with reference to all things," or "in every way." Growth must be balanced. When unity prevails in the Church, Christ being the true Head, then the members will grow in every respect in their relationship to Christ. It is sad, as Summers comments, "to see one who has grown physically but not mentally. . . . So is it sad to see one who has grown normally from every physical standard but spiritually he is as immature as a baby."[9] A growing church is one in which each member is experientially sound, evangelistically active, and doctrinally informed. That is the reason why these ministries are given to the Church.

When Christ is faithfully acknowledged as Head of the Church, and is given the right to rule the Church, He sees to it that *the whole body* is *fitly joined together and compacted* (16). From that harmonious relationship increase or growth occurs. Each separate part must do its share, too. When it supplies what it is designed to supply, the body functions normally and grows. So it is with the Church. As the human body possesses within itself that which enables it to mature, so the Church possesses within herself the dynamic presence of Christ who keeps the ministries functioning effectively, the result of which is growth in love.

The Old Life and the New
Ephesians 4:17-32

The Christians with whom Paul is corresponding "had been breathing from their childhood the foul atmosphere of a most corrupt form of heathenism; they were still breathing it."[1] Paul has no doubt that these people had come into a new life and he is ready to declare that fact. But he is also ready to lay on them the imperative to *walk not as other Gentiles walk* (17). In other words, "Conduct yourselves in such a way as to show everyone the real difference that exists between you and your pagan neighbors." Unquestionably they can live holy and blameless lives right where they are because Christ has given them a moral energy which, when released in obedience and faith to Him, will produce a life-style acceptable to God. Summers is correct when he observes that "if the religious experience with Christ professed by the individual does not correct the evil that was once in his life, either there is something wrong with the profession that the individual makes, or there is something wrong with his own application of life and purpose to that profession."[2] The previous section (1-16) dealt with the Church's unity, whereas this one deals with the Church's purity.

Life Without Christ

Ephesians 4:17-19

> 17 This I say therefore, and testify in the Lord, that ye henceforth walk not as other Gentiles walk, in the vanity of their mind,
> 18 Having the understanding darkened, being alienated from the life of God through the ignorance that is in them, because of the blindness of their heart:
> 19 Who being past feeling have given themselves over unto lasciviousness, to work all uncleanness with greediness.

Graphically, Paul describes the life of his readers before they came to Christ. What he writes here reminds us of the awesome description of the pagan world found in Rom. 1:21-32. Four descriptive phrases express the condition of these people. (1) They conducted their lives *in the vanity of their mind* (17), by which Paul means, "in futility and emptiness, without any sense of real purpose." Sensual satisfactions controlled their thinking and living. (2) Their *understanding darkened* means "to be without the faculty of discernment, to be unable to distinguish between right and wrong."[3] (3) They were *alienated from the life of God* (18), by which Paul means they were "dead in trespasses and sins" (2:1). This separation from God was due to their *ignorance* and the *blindness of their heart.* *Blindness* might be better translated "hardness" because in the original language the term used, taken from medical practice, suggests the hardening of the skin or the creation of a callous by constant contact with a foreign substance. Insensitivity to pain results. In this case incessant sinning brings about a hardening of the heart. (4) They were past the point of any moral feeling (19). Habitual sinning finally brought them to the place where they made a business of practicing immorality. They had "lost all decent feelings and abandoned themselves to sensuality, practising any form of impurity which lust can suggest" (19, Phillips).

We know that ancient society was debauched; history clearly records that fact. But before we engage in condemnation and judgment, we had better look at our own times. Sophisticated sensuality and hell-inspired evil abound everywhere. Both the ancient and the modern societies attest to the fact that life without Christ can and often does lead to such unrestrained wickedness.

Life with Christ

Ephesians 4:20-24

20 But ye have not so learned Christ;
21 If so be that ye have heard him, and have been taught by him, as the truth is in Jesus:
22 That ye put off concerning the former conversation the old man, which is corrupt according to the deceitful lusts;

23 And be renewed in the spirit of your mind;
24 And that ye put on the new man, which after God is created in righteousness and true holiness.

Once again in this Epistle we encounter the adversative conjunction "but" which introduces a picture in radical contrast to that which had just been painted by the Apostle. It speaks of the difference Christ has made in the life of these people. *But ye have not so learned Christ* (20) is an awkward statement. We would normally expect something like, "But ye have not been so taught about Christ." However, the Greek word for *learned* comes from the same root as the word *disciple*. A disciple is a learner, one who is being taught. It would seem that the Apostle is suggesting something about their having been discipled to Christ, or becoming a disciple of Christ. The clause in the next verse, *and have been taught by him* (21), supports this idea. Thus, their knowledge of the Christ-way, which is completely opposite to their old way of life, resulted from a living fellowship with Christ. E. F. Scott observes, "To be taught or *instructed in Christ* is not merely to be taught by him, or by the messenger who speaks in his name. It suggests an inward union with the divine Teacher."[4] Christ becomes therefore the ultimate criterion for evaluating all moral actions. The Spirit of Christ within becomes the Teacher of things holy and blameless.

1. *Life with Christ* means that one has *put off . . . the old man* (22). The King James Version is correct in its translation of the Greek. Some other versions translate verse 22 as an imperative; for example, "Put off your old nature" (RSV). However, what Paul is saying here is something like this: "When you were discipled to Christ, you put off your old man, and began to be renewed in your mind and to be clothed with the new man." *The old man* is the old way of life which is thrown off like an old garment. Col. 3:9-10 is a parallel statement: "Lie not one to another, seeing that ye have put off the old man with his deeds, and have put on the new man which is renewed (being

renewed, NASB) in knowledge after the image of him that created him" (see also Rom. 6:6). Newness in Paul is related to the initial experience of grace, as in the reference in 2 Cor. 5:17: "If any man be in Christ, he is a new creature: old things are passed away; behold, all things are become new."

When we come to Christ, we become new persons. The dynamic of His life lays hold of us and we are enabled to shed the filthy rags of sin and self-righteousness and appear in new robes as really new people. What we once were no longer exists. It is gone.

2. *Life with Christ* means that *the spirit of your mind* is being *renewed* day by day (23). "Putting off the old man" is instantaneous, but "being renewed in the spirit of one's mind" is continuous and progressive. A parallel Pauline verse is Rom. 12:2 which says, literally, "Continue to be transformed by the renewing of your mind." This is process and it suggests growth in the inner life. It is *the spirit of your mind* that is being renewed, suggesting that new moral understandings are developing as well as new moral actions taking place based upon radicalized spiritual thinking and willing. A. M. Hunter comments, "A true conversion will change a man's mental as well as his moral habits."[5]

3. *Life with Christ* means putting on a new nature (24). It is as Stott has suggested, "putting on new clothes." Putting on *the new man* is the counterpart of putting off *the old man* (22). The new nature, the new self, is created "after the likeness of God" (RSV), or "in Christlikeness" and manifests itself *in righteousness and true holiness.* When we put on Christ, who is "the new man of all men," the divine nature becomes operative in our lives (see Rom. 13:14; 1 Cor. 15:45 ff; Gal. 3:27). We are "partakers of the divine nature" (2 Pet. 1:4). When this happens, the twin traits of Christlikeness—righteousness and holiness—begin to appear in the life. Bruce concludes, "God himself is righteous and holy; His righteousness and holiness are

perfectly manifested in Christ, and those who put on Christ are accordingly characterized by righteousness and holiness."[6]

New-Life Injunctions

Ephesians 4:25-32

> 25 Wherefore putting away lying, speak every man truth with his neighbour: for we are members one of another.
> 26 Be ye angry, and sin not: let not the sun go down upon your wrath:
> 27 Neither give place to the devil.
> 28 Let him that stole steal no more: but rather let him labour, working with his hands the thing which is good, that he may have to give to him that needeth.
> 29 Let no corrupt communication proceed out of your mouth, but that which is good to the use of edifying, that it may minister grace unto the hearers.
> 30 And grieve not the holy Spirit of God, whereby ye are sealed unto the day of redemption.
> 31 Let all bitterness, and wrath, and anger, and clamour, and evil speaking, be put away from you, with all malice:
> 32 And be ye kind one to another, tenderhearted, forgiving one another, even as God for Christ's sake hath forgiven you.

What follows in the next eight verses is closely related to Paul's description of the new life in Christ. The word *wherefore* is the connection. In effect it says, "Now that you are new men, live your new lives in keeping with the following instructions." Having put off the old life and having put on the new life with its continued renewing of the mind, they are exhorted to throw off all conduct which characterized their old life and make their behavior consistent with the kind of persons they have become and are becoming. The new life has and must have a specific life-style. Working on this fundamental principle, Paul in rapid fashion sets forth five injunctions to which his readers must give earnest heed. Note should be taken of the fact that he singles out five sins and their opposite virtues. "It is not enough to put off the old rags; we have to put on new garments."[7]

1. *Don't tell lies, but rather tell the truth* (25).[8] Literally rendered, this injunction says, "Having put off the false-

hood, keep on speaking truth." Lying disrupts the fellowship of the Christian community, so the truth must be spoken with exacting consistency.

2. *Don't lose your temper, but rather be sure that your anger is righteous* (26-27). Apparently there are two kinds of anger, righteous and unrighteous. The former is consistent with the Christlike life, as we see in our Lord's experience of cleansing the Temple (Mark 3:5; John 2:13-17). "Sinless anger is the mark of moral nature under the control of ethical love."[9] Anger that arises out of wounded pride or the like, however, is sinful. Anger becomes sin whenever it desires, or is willing, to harm someone.

But even righteous indignation has its dangers. Thus, Paul counsels: *Let not the sun go down upon your wrath* (26). In other words, "Don't go to sleep at night, or let a day pass, without engaging in the necessary activity to reduce the heat of your anger." Furthermore, allowance should not be given to the devil to do his destructive work in one's relationship with others by one's failure to bring his anger under control.

3. *Don't steal, but rather work and give* (28). Christians live by the Ten Commandments, and the eighth one forbids stealing. Community health cannot be maintained whenever a thief is at work in the group. Stealing includes all forms of theft, even the stealing of time from one's employer. Paul exhorts the Christian to become an honest workman so that he may have material resources *to give to him that needeth.* The background of this injunction is the obvious responsibility of the church to care for the welfare of each member.

4. *Don't use your mouth for evil but rather for good* (29-30). What distinguishes man from all other of God's creatures is his ability to speak. Speech is a marvelous gift. However, out of the mouth of man can proceed both good and evil. Paul uses a special word to express *corrupt communication.* It means that which is rotten and is used

of trees which produce rotten fruit (see Matt. 7:17-18; 12:33). Good speech is of a character that builds up the body of believers and convicts the hearts of sinners. Edifying speech is both gracious and a means of grace. It has been said that "Christian conversation ought to be such that it can be listened to with pleasure and at the same time be religiously helpful." After Jesus completed His exposition of Isaiah 61 in His hometown synagogue in Nazareth, the people "were surprised that words of such grace should fall from his lips" (Luke 4:22, NEB).

The reference to grieving the Holy Spirit at first might appear to be out of context. But if we understand that the Spirit is the Spirit of Truth, we gain some insight into the Apostle's intention. When our speech is fraught with falsehood and unkindness, and does not contribute to the building up of the Body of Christ, the Spirit, who is personal, is grieved. His work is that of creating a holy people, and when our words are less than gracious, that is, having no redeeming or holiness-creating character, He sorrows. Having been stamped with His nature, we should conduct our lives in keeping with His desires and purposes.

5. *Don't be unkind or bitter, but rather kind and loving* (31-32). The cluster of evil characteristics given in verse 31 are descriptive of the old nature, while those listed in verse 32 depict the new nature. An internal relationship exists among the four evil traits mentioned in verse 31. *Bitterness* (a highly irritated state of mind, a sour spirit, unwilling to be reconciled) often leads to *wrath* (fury), which in turn produces *anger* (a settled spirit of retaliation), which finally provokes *clamour* (excited, loud speaking) and *evil speaking* (slander, blasphemy). *Malice* (bad feeling, ill will) is "the spring of the faults which have been enumerated." A depraved spirit will produce "the works of the flesh," about which Paul speaks in Gal. 5:19-21. It is evident that the Apostle is depicting an extreme mode of behavior, but he does so in order to dramatize how the unity of the body can be quickly destroyed by unholy living.

He appeals finally to the example of God in Christ Jesus in dealing with us. We should treat others in the same manner that God has treated us, with kindness, tenderheartedness, and forgiveness (32). Here we touch the very heart of the Christian ethic, namely, the attitude and conduct of God toward us. The Golden Rule, "Do unto others as you would have them do unto you," applied outside the experience of God's abounding grace toward us, would only be an exhortation to ineffective human, moral effort. Put within the context of God's forgiving and merciful disposition toward us, the rule, when followed faithfully, becomes the basis of maintaining peace and unity in the body of believers, the church, and in the world at large.

Living as the Beloved

Ephesians 5:1-21

EPHESIANS 5

On the basis of the forgoing exhortations as to how they should live out the life with Christ, and more specifically, how to function properly in the church, Paul makes a fresh appeal to his readers to be *followers of God, as dear children* ("beloved children," RSV). This tender reference to their relationship to God indicates the deep feeling of Paul concerning the development of their spiritual lives. They are "God's dear children" (NEB) because they have responded to His overtures of grace and have been adopted into His family. However, Paul gently reminds them that they must live a life commensurate with their nature as children of God. They must continue "living as the beloved."[1]

The term "walk" appears again in the imperative form. The readers are exhorted to conduct their lives in keeping with the divine purposes and example. "Living as the beloved" involves (1) walking worthy of our calling, 4:1; (2) walking in a manner different from the Gentiles, 4:17; (3) walking in love, 5:2; (4) walking in light, 5:8; (5) walking in wisdom, 5:15. The last three in this grouping come to expression in chapter 5.

Walking in Love

Ephesians 5:1-7

> 1 Be ye therefore followers of God as dear children:
> 2 And walk in love, as Christ also hath loved us, and hath given himself for us an offering and a sacrifice to God for a sweetsmelling savour.
> 3 But fornication, and all uncleanness, or covetousness, let it not be once named among you, as becometh saints;
> 4 Neither filthiness, nor foolish talking, nor jesting, which are not convenient: but rather giving of thanks.
> 5 For this ye know, that no whoremonger, nor unclean person, nor covetous man, who is an idolater, hath any inheritance in the kingdom of Christ and of God.
> 6 Let no man deceive you with vain words: for because of these things cometh the wrath of God upon the children of disobedience.
> 7 Be not ye therefore partakers with them.

The call to walk in love is a parallel idea to the call to be *followers* (imitators) *of God*. They cannot copy the essence or activity of God, such as His work as Creator or Redeemer, or His Trinity, but they are called "to imitate his love and make progress on the way of love."[2] Not any other person's model behavior, nor any philosophical ideal will suffice for this imitation. God the Father and Christ the Son together constitute the model. Mackay concludes that to "copy God" is "to be like a Person, to reflect His image" and not simply to be loyal to truth or even "loyal to loyalty."[3] God is love, and because He acts in keeping with His nature, He acts lovingly toward all men.

Earlier the Apostle prayed that they would be "rooted

and grounded in love" (3:17), that they would speak "the truth in love" (4:15), and that their behavior would be such as to build up the church "in love" (4:16). Now he counsels them to make their whole lives a reflection—indeed, a demonstration—of the love of God. Salmond comments, "The 'imitation' must take effect in the practical, unmistakable form of a loving course in life."[4] This love which is to unfold in the life is not a natural human love, but agapeic love—that which is God-given. It is pure self-giving; it asks nothing in return, and it wishes only for the well-being of the one on whom it is showered.

1. *The pattern of love which is to be the essence of the Christian's walk is found in the sacrifice of Christ.* Both the reality and possibility of walking in *agape* love are portrayed in Christ. Three declarations concerning Christ's pattern for us are made.

   a. Christ also hath loved us, and hath given himself for us (2). The fact of His love for us is the starting point of the gospel. But that is not enough. His love led Him to sacrifice himself for us. This love issued in a priceless gift, namely, the gift of himself at Calvary. True love acts profoundly and surprisingly!

   b. The gift of himself was *an offering and sacrifice,* which, given the Old Testament background and Paul's other teachings, refers to Christ's bloody death for the sins of mankind. The imitation called for is not necessarily that of dying on a cross, but that of appropriating by faith His love so as to be able to share it fully, and at whatever cost, with one's fellow Christians and with others in spiritual need.

   c. The sacrifice of Christ was a *sweetsmelling savour* to God. As Barth has made clear, in the Old Testament system, to offer a sacrifice was not enough; the sacrifice must be acceptable to God by having come from a heart truly obedient to Him. Proper performance of the sacrifice was not enough. An offering may have some value for the worshipper but "its value to God depends on whether God is pleased with the offerer and his gift."[5] The aroma of Christ's gift of himself at Calvary brought pleasure to God.

Our love must partake of this love of Christ. If we genuinely imitate God, we will love others with something of the same passionate, unselfish, sacrifical love that motivated the heart of our Lord. Suffering with Him will be reflected in that love.

2. *The perversion of the love-walk is an ever-present possibility* (3-4). Paul always saw things in contrast. The grand thought of the pure love of Christ leads him spontaneously to see the other side, the life no longer directed by love. Love's perversion is seen in six sins: *(a) fornication* (immorality); *(b) uncleanness* (sensual indulgence); *(c) coveteousness* (greed); *(d) filthiness* (filthy talk); *(e) foolish talking* (silly talk); *(f) jesting* (coarse, ribald talk). When Paul comments that such talk is *not conveninent,* he means it is "not fitting" (RSV) or "out of place" (NEB). These sinful patterns of conduct are unbecoming to those who claim to be conducting their lives in love, for in every case these forms of conduct are blatant contradictions of the law of God and they destroy the unity of the church.

On the contrary, God's dear children should have thanksgiving in their hearts and on their lips often. As Scott says, "The conversation of Christians ought always to have in it something of that thanksgiving which is the distinctive mood of the Christian life."[6] Perhaps we should see this note on thanksgiving as suggesting a proper attitude toward sex. Paul is setting the Christian view of sex over against the pagan view which permitted promiscuity and vulgar talk. Sex is a gift of God, for which we should be thankful and which should not be downgraded by jesting.

3. *The penalties of this perversion of the unity which love is to create among God's people are two in number* (5-7): *(a) No inheritance in the kingdom of Christ and of God* (5), and *(b)* Liability to *the wrath of God* (6). Persons who indulge in such evil practice do not now enjoy the life of the

Kingdom and will not enjoy it in the future if they do not change their ways. In fact, at the present time they are living under the heavy hand of the wrath of God. Already they are objects of its fury (see 2:3) but in the last day they will feel its full retribution. God is righteous and His kingdom is one of righteousness (Rom. 14:17) and the unrighteous cannot enter it.

Two exhortations are simultaneously given. The first cautions the readers not to let anyone *deceive* them *with vain words* (6), that is to say, they are not to fall prey to the shallow arguments of those who insist that these vices will not affect their personal relationships with Christ and thus the church. It may well be that Paul has in mind a group called the Gnostics, who claimed that bodily sins could be committed without damaging the soul and without impurity. The second exhortation is a directive that they *be not . . . partakers with* such people, for they are really *children of disobedience* (6-7; see 2 Cor. 6:14—7:1).

Walking in Light

Ephesians 5:8-14

> 8 For ye were sometimes darkness, but now are ye light in the Lord: walk as children of light:
> 9 (For the fruit of the Spirit is in all goodness and righteousness and truth;)
> 10 Proving what is acceptable unto the Lord.
> 11 And have no fellowship with the unfruitful works of darkness, but rather reprove them.
> 12 For it is a shame even to speak of those things which are done of them in secret.
> 13 But all things that are reproved are made manifest by the light: for whatsoever doth make manifest is light.
> 14 Wherefore he saith, Awake thou that sleepest, and arise from the dead, and Christ shall give thee light.

1. *God's children are to walk as children of light* (8). Love is the dynamic of the Christian life but light gives it direction. Once the Ephesians *were sometimes darkness* but now are *light in the Lord.* At one time they not only groped in darkness; they were part of the darkness as well as contributors to it. Now they are partakers of the light

and contributors to it. Jesus spoke of himself as "the light of the world," by which He meant that His life flooded the world with the truth about God. He illuminated the minds of men so they could understand the fatherly and forgiving nature of God and His eternal purposes of redemption (see John 1:4-5; 3:19; 9:5; 12:36).

All who believe in Him, therefore, are bathed with light and now can comprehend the deep things of God. Jesus said: "I am the light of the world: he that followeth me shall not walk in darkness, but shall have the light of life" (John 8:12). All who refuse to follow Him are left in darkness, which, with the passing of the years, becomes more impenetrable. So the exhortation of Paul to his readers is, "As children of God, express your true nature and live according to the new understanding of spiritual things you have received from Christ." "Possessing light" or "being in the light" also denotes the operation of God's grace in the life unto holy living. Jesus spoke of having the "whole body . . . full of light, having no part dark" (Luke 11:34-36).

2. *The fruit of walking in the light* is threefold in nature: *goodness and righteousness and truth* (9). Paul's declarations on the character of true Christians are usually followed by statements of the Christians' ethical responsibility. "Fruit" indicates "the moral significance of *light,* as against false mystical interpretations, or any boast of 'enlightenment' which was barren of moral effect."[7] Any false teachers, like the Gnostics, who boasted of special insight into spiritual matters but decried any moral responsibility, are dead wrong. To walk in love is to walk in light and to have a serious concern for ethical integrity.

3. *The "light" in which the children of God walk must be constantly tested, much in the way that the quality of metals needs repeated testing* (10). Paul wants his readers to conduct their lives in a morally discriminating manner and this requires that they put all their actions "to the test of acceptability" *unto the Lord,* that is, unto Christ.

Correspondence between the pattern of behavior and the perfect will of God is absolutely necessary. The Holy Spirit is available to assist one in knowing God's will and actualizing it in life.

4. *When the children of God "walk in light" they also reprove the "unfruitful works of darkness"* (11-13). Such works are *unfruitful* because they produce no goodness. The reproof expected of light-filled Christians takes on the character of exposure. When the God-given light falls on the practices of sinners, it reveals the unspiritual nature of their lives. This reproof comes either by word or deed. Scott assumes the latter:

> As a rule, when we speak of exposing an evil we think of denouncing it, as loudly and publicly as we can. Paul's idea is that of a silent process, comparable to the action of light. . . . By living a life which is unquestionably pure and right he (the Christian) will reveal the heathen vices as they really are, and this will be the most effective way of "rebuking" them.[8]

Probably we should understand that the Christian must be prepared to reprove the works of darkness in whatever manner is most appropriate at the time. However, one's word must certainly be supported by righteous deeds.

Verse 12 states why the works of darkness must be exposed. First, because of their exceeding sinfulness, *for it is a shame even to speak of those things.* Second, because of their hiddenness, for they are done *in secret.* Sin begets sin and its reproductive powers must be destroyed. In verse 13 Paul suggests the possibility of transforming the dark deeds into the qualities of light. The idea here rests upon the principle that once the light shines the darkness disappears. So Beare concludes that "the power of the light not only reveals, but penetrates and transforms into its own likeness whatever it illuminates."[9] We must believe that the steady shining of a pure life on a darkened soul or society will, first of all, bring shame and then, hopefully, purity.

5. *The light which God's children enjoy is a gift* (14). This verse concludes Paul's appeal to "walk in the light." Many interpreters consider this verse to be an early Christian hymn because of its poetic form and assume that it was sung at Christian baptisms. In cases where pagans were being baptized it symbolized "the emergence of the new Christian from the dark sweep of paganism into the radiant and awakening light of the Christian way."[10] Perhaps Paul is reminding his readers of their own experience of turning from darkness unto light and, with that reminder, is urging them to continue to walk in the light, not only for their own personal salvation but also for the salvation of others.

Walking in Wisdom

Ephesians 5:15-21

> 15 See then that ye walk circumspectly, not as fools, but as wise,
> 16 Redeeming the time, because the days are evil.
> 17 Wherefore be ye not unwise, but understanding what the will of the Lord is.
> 18 And be not drunk with wine, wherein is excess; but be filled with the Spirit;
> 19 Speaking to yourselves in psalms and hymns and spiritual songs, singing and making melody in your heart to the Lord;
> 20 Giving thanks always for all things unto God and the Father in the name of our Lord Jesus Christ;
> 21 Submitting yourselves one to another in the fear of God.

The relationship of this section to the preceding context presents a problem. Bouncing off verse 14 with its special appeal to continue walking the path of light, Paul exhorts his readers not to live carelessly in the evil environment in which they find themselves. Wisdom should direct their lives. The key thought therefore is, *"walk circumspectly, not as fools, but as wise* (15). The word *circumspectly* is an enchanting one. Literally it means "exactly," or "by rule," that is, "according to a set of established norms." In effect, Paul is exhorting them to walk carefully, or, as the English word *circumspectly* suggests, "looking all around." *Wise* Christians are those whose minds and hearts are illuminated by the divine light or with the divine mind, thus giving a divine perspective on the issues of right and wrong.

Paul now indicates various ways by which the walk in wisdom is evidenced.

1. *Redeeming the time* (16). Phillips' rendering of this verse is well known: "Make the best use of your time, despite all the evils of these days." *Time,* in this instance, includes also the concept of opportunity. Paul is exhorting the wise person to "grasp the opportunity to serve God" in these critical and corrupt days. Just as a commercial buyer, who knows the market, will close what promises to be a good deal immediately, so the Christian will readily take advantage of God's grace to enable him to be of service. "Opportunities for Christian service are brief seasons that soon slip by. The wise Christian will recognize them and use them while he can."[11]

2. *Understanding the will of God* (17). It has been said that the primary concern of the Christian must be to discern the will of God and to do it. Who would doubt that such is the way of wisdom?

3. *Being filled with the Spirit* (18). Behind this exhortation may be a reminder of the drunken revelries of the mystery religions to which these new Christians may have once been adherents. Drunkenness for Paul is "the gateway to profligacy" *(excess).* "The Christian gets his 'lift' from the Divine Spirit, not from distilled spirits." Full control of one's person is in keeping with the nature of Christian holiness. *But be filled with the Spirit* is the heart of Paul's thought here. *Be filled* is in the present tense and should be translated "be continually filled with the Spirit." It stands to reason that a Christian cannot go on being filled with the Spirit until he has first been filled at some given time, as was the experience of the early disciples on the Day of Pentecost. The imperative here, therefore, is not related to the initial experience of sanctification but rather to keeping oneself submissive to the

ministry of the Spirit. Not only is there a specific time when the Holy Spirit comes to fill the heart, cleansing it and endowing it with love, there is also the moment-by-moment filling as the Christian lives in close relationship with the Spirit.

4. *Expressing the Spirit's joy* (19-20). A Spirit-filled life is expressed in spiritual songs, joyous fellowship, and gratitude to God. The Spirit creates this hilarious, joyful spirit in the life of God's people. The music of the Spirit-filled life is normal, varied *(psalms and hymns and spiritual songs),* and heart-created ("making music in your hearts for the ears of the Lord," Phillips). A constant note sounded in authentic Christian music is thanksgiving: *giving thanks always for all things* (20, see Col. 3:17; 1 Thess. 1:2; 5:18). *All things* puzzles us, for some experiences in life hardly provide the basis for joy. The qualifying phrase *in the name of our Lord Jesus Christ* suggests that our thanks should rest, not upon the immediate circumstances, but upon the knowledge of the sustained fatherly care of God and the hope of the final redemption of all things through the work of our Lord Jesus Christ.

5. *Submitting to one another* (21). Life in the Spirit leads the Christian community finally to the submitting *one to another in the fear of God.* The Greek word expressing *submitting yourselves one to another* is a present middle participle *(hypotassomenoi)* which denotes mutual submission or consideration. Nothing of authoritarianism or hyper-individualism, demanding "personal rights," is suggested here. Such attitudes eventually destroy the unity of the fellowship. Reverence for (fear of) God, who through His Spirit brought the Church into existence, will temper all that the Christian thinks, speaks, and does within the body of believers. There is no place for unholy aggressiveness, self-assertiveness, and arrogance. As Stott reminds us, the Holy Spirit is "a humble Spirit, and those who are truly filled with him always display the meekness and gentleness of Christ. It is one of their most evident char-

acteristics that they submit to one another."[12] Thus, this submission to one another is voluntary, personal, and has full ethical value for the one who submits himself and for others whom he serves in spiritual surrender.

Christian Relationships
Ephesians 5:22—6:9

The instruction to be submissive to one another in verse 21 governs the thought in the next three paragraphs having to do with wives and husbands (22-33), children and parents (6:1-4), and masters and slaves (6:5-9). These are really examples of the general concept of meaningful, Christian relationships enunciated in verse 21.

Two principles control Paul's discourse on these "household duties" or domestic relations. The *first* is "the far-reaching precept of mutual subjection." While in each set of associations the one person is asked to submit in one way or another, the second person, on the other hand, is charged with exacting responsibilities. The law of reciprocal duties is applicable in each case. The *second* principle is that "the obligation is based on the connection of the believer with Christ (5:22; 6:1, 5)."[1]

"Being in the Lord" finally governs this kind of interpersonal living. Submission to one another in the family is not of the same degree as that which one is called upon to make to the Lord. However, the expected mutual submission and love finds its model and dynamic in the relationship which exists between the Christian and the Lord. If the forgiving, cleansing grace of God flourishes in the heart of the Christian, it follows that grace will infuse and bless all the normal relationships of life and, most assuredly, the domestic relationships. If reconciliation with God, the exchange of an old set of relationships for a new set of relationships, has really occurred in the life through the power of the gospel, then the whole of life has been renewed and the family relationships partake of the peace of that reconciliation.

A concluding introductory word is appropriate here. Four aspects of this discussion must be kept steadily in mind:

1. The exhortations to obedience and submission do not mean that some persons are in any way inferior.

2. Paul was as sensitive to the worth of a person as was our Lord. As Stott suggests, Jesus and His apostles, Paul included, affirmed *(a)* the *dignity* of womanhood, childhood and servanthood; *(b)* the *equality* before God of all human beings, irrespective of race, rank, class, culture, sex, or age; and *(c)* the deeper *unity* of all Christian believers, as fellow members of God's family and of Christ's Body.[2]

3. The differences we see in these relationships is not the difference of personhood but of roles played by persons in the existing social structure. We are not talking about male and female, for instance, but rather about the roles of wife and husband. The same is true with regard to children and fathers, and slaves and masters. With the assumption of particular social roles there comes a degree of authority, as a gift from God. But the authority of a role in no way brings greater worth to the person. Under God, all are equal, but some persons have specific functions in life which demand levels of authority. Those who do not fill that role must acknowledge the authority of the one in that role and become submissive or obedient to him in order that he may fulfill the God-given responsibilities of that role.

4. One must follow Paul's arguments carefully. He enunciates three in particular: *(a)* The *Christological argument,* the strongest one, which implies that both "the supposedly high and the supposedly low are subordinated to the same highest authority." Before the Lord all are

equal and all must obey (6:1, 4-7, 9); *(b)* The *eschato-logical argument* which asserts that all will be brought to judgment. "Sweating slaves and threatening masters alike are to live now as people determined by the future"; *(c)* The *practical argument* which emphasizes what is "right" and "good" (6:8).[3]

The Relationship of Husbands and Wives

Ephesians 5:22-33

> 22 Wives, submit yourselves unto your own husbands, as unto the Lord.
> 23 For the husband is the head of the wife, even as Christ is the head of the church: and he is the saviour of the body.
> 24 Therefore as the church is subject unto Christ, so let the wives be to their own husbands in every thing.
> 25 Husbands, love your wives, even as Christ also loved the church, and gave himself for it;
> 26 That he might sanctify and cleanse it with the washing of water by the word,
> 27 That he might present it to himself a glorious church, not having spot, or wrinkle, or any such thing; but that it should be holy and without blemish.
> 28 So ought men to love their wives as their own bodies. He that loveth his wife loveth himself.
> 29 For no man ever yet hated his own flesh; but nourisheth and cherisheth it, even as the Lord the church:
> 30 For we are members of his body, of his flesh, and of his bones.
> 31 For this cause shall a man leave his father and mother, and shall be joined unto his wife, and they two shall be one flesh.
> 32 This is a great mystery: but I speak concerning Christ and the church.
> 33 Nevertheless let every one of you in particular so love his wife even as himself; and the wife see that she reverence her husband.

Ideally, the effects of a changed life will reach into society, the church, and the home. The home, and especially the marital relationship, constitutes the major test of the transforming and reconciling power of the gospel. Paul's concern here is with the relationship between husbands and wives, and his directives are essentially two: *(a)* Wives, be submissive to your own husbands; *(b)* Husbands, love your wives.

1. The duty of wives is to *submit yourselves unto your own husbands as unto the Lord* (22; see 1 Cor. 11:2-16; Col. 3:18-19; Titus 2:4-5; 1 Pet. 3:1-7).

a. Paul is not referring to wives simply as females; rather his injunction to subordination relates to their roles as wives. Male and female are created equal in every respect, but in the marital setting the husband has certain divinely ordained prerogatives and his wife should recognize them and gladly accept them, otherwise chaos will prevail in the home.

b. This voluntary submission is done *as unto the Lord,* since it is the Lord who has given this authority to the husband. Submission to the Lord should readily lead wives to submission to their husbands, since it is the Lord's authority their husbands exercise.

c. In Paul's theological system there exists "a chain of relationships" (23). First Corinthians 11:3 gives succinct expression to it: "I want you to understand that the head of every man is Christ, the head of a woman is her husband, and the head of Christ is God" (RSV). The order is God, Christ, man, and woman. Beare discerns two elements in this system: (1) headship "denotes primarily controlling authority and the right to obedience." (2) Control and obedience take place "within a living organism where the two parts are complementary to the other."[4] Furthermore, as Christ is the Head of the Church, so the husband is head of the wife. Christ, unquestionably, has the best interest of the Church at heart and so does the true husband of the wife. Christ is the *saviour of the body,* namely, the Church, and analogously, the husband is the deliverer and protector of his wife. Any sacrifice on his part that creates a sense of well-being and security will in turn evoke free and loving submission from his wife.

d. Just as the Church must give herself without reserve to her Lord if she is to enjoy the peaceful life, so the wife must give herself to her husband *in every thing* (24). The little phrase, *in every thing,* might be offensive to wives in contemporary society who carry heavy responsibilities as mothers as well as in vocations outside the home. What should be her attitude when conflicts arise?

The answer is a matter of priorities. Foulkes remarks: "She may fulfill any function and any responsibility in society, but if she has accepted before God the responsibility of marriage and of a family, these must be her first concern."[5]

It must be clearly understood, however, that when there is a flagrant misuse or abuse of authority by the husband, the wife is no longer obligated to submit. A husband and wife who claim relationship to Christ should restablish their priorities and should be prepared to give major attention to any problems of misunderstanding and of decision-making which arise in the fulfillment of their daily responsibilities. Unity in love must be their first and highest goal.

2. *The duty of husbands* is to love their wives with a love like unto the love of Christ for His bride, the Church (25-33). The obligations of the husbands are every bit as demanding as those of the wives. Speaking to the husbands, St. Chrysostom exhorted: "Hast thou seen the measure of obedience? hear also the measure of love. Wouldst thou that thy wife should obey thee as the Church doth Christ? have care thyself for her, as Christ for the Church." Paul puts the imperative *love* in the present tense, thereby emphasizing the need for continuous, unabating, growing loving. The love which brought the wife to the husband initially must be daily nurtured and expressed to his lover. The model to be emulated is Christ's love for His Church—sacrificing, sanctifying, sustaining, and caring.

a. *Christ's love was a self-giving love* (25). Christ *gave himself for it* (see Gal. 1:4; Titus 2:14). Earlier in verse 2 Paul appealed to his readers to "walk in love, as Christ also hath loved us, and hath given himself for us." The norm for everything Christian is Christ and His willingness to give himself at Calvary for our salvation. Following an example is not the sum total of Paul's thought here, so that the exhortation rests merely on moral persuasion.

More specifically, it rests on a moral change of personhood. Christ's death brought a new life to the husbands, a life free from the bondage of sin. It was a love that changed their inner lives. Now that they share in that divine love, they must allow it to control and guide their relationships with their wives. If they do, they will be willing to make any sacrifices to keep the relationships pure and stable. Bruce's word is judicious and must be heard by both husbands and wives. "By setting this highest of standards for the husband's treatment of his wife, Paul goes to the limit in safeguarding the wife's dignity and welfare."[6]

b. Christ's love was a sanctifying love (26-27). The object of Christ's great gift of himself in death on the Cross was the sanctification of the Church. The benefits of that ignominious act were not to be for himself but were to accrue finally to His people. Note should be taken of the fact that our biblical text says that Christ died that He might *sanctify and cleanse* the Church. A better rendering of the original language is "that He might sanctify her, having cleansed her" (NASB). The sentence structure in the Greek indicates that the experience referred to in the clause, "having cleansed her," preceded the sanctifying, and denotes the initial sanctification which takes place in conversion.

The love of Christ has as its ultimate purpose the full or entire sanctification of the Church, an experience subsequent to the initial cleansing of conversion. "Wherefore Jesus also, that he might sanctify the people with his own blood, suffered without the gate" (Heb. 13:12). His purifying love works a beauty in the Church until it is *a glorious church, not having spot, or wrinkle, or any such thing* (27). It is a Church that is *holy and without blemish* (see 1:4). Christ presents the Church *to himself.* "Bridegroom love" creates the beauty of the bride. When the Church goes forth into the world, she goes with a beauty of holiness originating in the sacrifical love of her Lord. So will it be with the wife whose husband's love possesses something of this sacrificial quality!

c. *Christ's love was a sustaining and caring love* (28-31). Returning to his central concern, namely, the husband-wife relationship, Paul declares that husbands ought *to love their wives as their own bodies* (28). Love of the physical body as such is not the full thrust of the thought here. Rather, husbands should love their wives "as being their own bodies; as part of their total self, not as another being external to them."[7] Husband and wife are "complementary parts of one personality." Verse 31 supports this interpretation: *For this cause shall a man leave his father and mother, and shall be joined unto his wife, and they shall be one flesh.* When this oneness pervades the thought and spirit of the husband, he will instinctively sustain, protect, and tenderly care for his wife, *for no man ever yet hated his own flesh; but nourisheth and cherisheth it, even as the Lord the church* (29).

Flesh in this verse means "self" or "being." Naturally, the physical side of life is incorporated in this thought because it is a significant part of the whole. The husband feeds and clothes his body but he also develops his mind and cares for all the relationships which comprise, and give meaning to, his existence. Just as Christ cares deeply for the totality of the Church's existence in the world, so should the husband care deeply and provide for the well-being of his wife's whole existence—body, mind, and spirit.

d. *Christ's love is a mystery* (32-33). Paul has been so caught up in the wonders and glories of Christ's union with His Church, he has found it difficult to keep in mind his original thought. At this point he writes, *This is a great mystery* (32), that is, the relationship between *Christ and the church.* However, the mystical relationship between Christ and His Church is symbolic of the mystical relationship between husbands and wives. Both sets of relationships have this quality by virtue of the divine revelation which creates and preserves them. No doubt some of

Paul's readers will question his view of marriage, given the low status of women in both Gentile and Jewish societies. So Summers concludes, "When Paul said that the man is to exercise such loving care for his wife that he gives her interest first place and his own interest second place, he was indeed speaking a great mystery. He insists, however, that he is giving a distinctively Christian view of marriage. That is one of the wonders of revelation which God has given through the Christian religion."[8]

Verse 33 summarizes the husband's duty toward his wife and the wife's duty toward her husband. In essence, let each husband love his wife as himself, and let each wife reverence her husband. The love a husband has for his wife sacrifices and serves with a view to enabling her to become what God has designed for her. Her submission and respect in response to his love enables him to be and do what his husband role demands, namely, to exercise his God-given authority for the well-being of the marital relationship (see 1 Pet. 3:1-7).

EPHESIANS 6

The Relationship of Parents and Children

Ephesians 6:1-4

> 1 Children, obey your parents in the Lord: for this is right.
> 2 Honour thy father and mother; which is the first commandment with promise;
> 3 That it may be well with thee, and thou mayest live long on the earth.
> 4 And, ye fathers, provoke not your children to wrath: but bring them up in the nurture and admonition of the Lord.

When Christian love prevails in the home, a wholesome and satisfying life develops for all members of the home. The second most important dimension of the domestic structure is that of the relationship of parents to their children. The Bible's view of the worth of the child was in direct opposition to the attitude of the Gentile world for the most part. A father's power over a child in that day was awesome. He could punish a child mercilessly, or even sell the child into slavery if he thought such action were financially advantageous or he felt the child were worthless to him. Child life was cheap. Against such devaluation of young human life, Jesus when He called the children to himself, spoke of them as illustrative of the spirit which gains a person admission to the kingdom of God. (Matt. 19:14). Paul stands with Jesus and offers a truly Christian view of the relationship which should prevail between children and their parents.

1. Children are exhorted to *obey your parents in the Lord, for this is right* (1).

a. Obedience is the key word. Note that wives are called to submission while children are called to obey. As the Greek word suggests, obedience involves listening or paying attention to the one giving directions. Moreover, being in the present tense, the verb *obey* urges continuous or habitual conduct—"keep on obeying" or "make a habit of obeying." Much of the conflict in homes today is due to the unwillingness of children to "listen to reason." Not many parents have the capability to answer all the questions, or respond to all the "whys" of a child, but, for the most part, they can offer some insights into correct behavior because of their own experiences in life. It is imperative, nevertheless, that lines of communication be kept open by both parties, so that proper conduct will result and the tragedies of disobedience not occur.

b. Once again Paul sets this exhortation in the context of grace by using the little phrase *in the Lord* (see 5:22). Paul is talking, no doubt, to Christian parents and children. "In your understanding of the Christian way and your commitment to Christ" must be the meaning of this phrase. Obedience to parents is to be continuous and habitual in the context of the larger rule of Christ in the family. Nothing is said regarding obedience to directives which are clearly unchristian, but we would not be mis-interpreting Paul by suggesting that such action would not be condoned by him. In all likelihood he would not give instruction to disobedience unless there was a distinct conflict between the parents' directive and the gospel demands.

c. The sanctions for habitual obedience on the part of children are two in number. *First,* because it is *right,* that is, "righteous" or "well pleasing unto the Lord" (Col. 3:20). *Second,* because the fifth commandment enjoins it —*Honor thy father and thy mother* (Exod. 20:12; Deut. 5:16). Salmond comments, *"Obedience* is the *duty; honour* is the *disposition* of which obedience is born."[9] Moreover, this commandment speaks of the law of childhood and for that reason it is of chief or first importance. Also, it contains a promise of well-being and long life (3). Christi-anity is not a "prosperity" cult, offering primarily health, wealth, and long life. But we must not lose sight of the impact of faithfulness to God and good relations upon one's existence. As Theodore Wedel observes, "There simply are rewards that come to the godly—nonmaterial, if rightly seen, but no less humanly concrete."[10]

d. Should a child always obey his parents? Stott's answer is proper. "I think I need first to say that during a young person's minority . . . obedience to parents should be the norm, and disobedience the rare exception."[11] What should be the attitude of children who have reached their majority? They should honor their parents, never for-getting or neglecting them. American society may be dis-covering shortly the rightness of this commandment, as our parents, to whom we owe so much, suffer financial hardship due to inflation and economic turmoil in the world. Our attitudes and actions are far less commend-able than those of peoples of other lands where parenthood is still, to a large extent, revered.

2. Fathers are exhorted not to *provoke their children to wrath:* but to *bring them up in the nurture and admonition*

of the Lord (4). The instructions of Paul are always mutual in nature. First, he calls the children to obedience, but follows that instruction with counsels for the fathers, who bear the responsibilities of rearing the children.

a. There must be no provocation of the children to wrath, that is to say, to excite "the bad passions of their children by severity, injustice, partiality, or unreasonable exercise of authority."[12] Oppressive treatment will anger a child. Sometimes it is necessary, when correcting a child, to endure the child's displeasure. A parent should not fear that reaction. Rather, he or she should fear overcorrection. To avoid that result, the parent should be prayerful and attuned to the ministry of the Spirit who will give grace and wisdom as needed.

b. The *positive word* for the fathers is that they should bring the children up *in the nurture and admonition of the Lord. Nurture* can be taken to mean "discipline" or "general instruction." *Admonition* has the thrust of specific instruction. The task of fathers is to involve themselves in a serious and consistent program of training, including chastisement at times, in all those areas of life which will bring about personal, social, and spiritual growth. The little phrase *of the Lord* can be taken to mean "with a sense of responsibility to the Lord," or "in the mind and the spirit of the Lord." Both are important. If the second prevails, the first will likely develop. Findlay reminds us that "the child's 'obedience in the Lord' is its response to 'the discipline and admonition *of the Lord* exercised by its parents.'"[13] Furthermore, the parent stands between Christ and the child and his action will either make or mar the child's spiritual future.

The Relationship of Masters and Slaves

Ephesians 6:5-9

> 5 Servants, be obedient to them that are your masters according to the flesh, with fear and trembling, in singleness of your heart, as unto Christ;
> 6 Not with eyeservice, as menpleasers; but as the servants of Christ, doing the will of God from the heart;

> 7 With good will doing service, as to the Lord, and not to men:
> 8 Knowing that whatsoever good thing any man doeth, the same shall he receive of the Lord, whether he be bond or free.
> 9 And, ye masters, do the same things unto them, forbearing threatening: knowing that your Master also is in heaven; neither is there respect of persons with him.

Slavery was an awesome problem in the first century. It has been estimated that there were 60 million slaves in the Roman Empire alone. Not only unskilled laborers, but many doctors, teachers, secretaries, artists, as well as persons working in the government were owned as slaves. Christians in a free society might wonder why Paul and Peter did not attack this serious social problem. Their writings include only instructions to the slaves and masters as to how they should treat one another (see Col. 3:22-25; 1 Pet. 2:18-25).

There is not one command in Paul's writings calling for the release of slaves. Why? Several answers have been offered for this query. (1) Paul expected the soon return of the Lord and thus decided nothing could be gained by promoting such a massive change. (2) To encourage the emancipation of slaves "would have been to confirm the suspicion of many people in authority that the gospel aimed at the subversion of society."[14] (3) The economic status of slaves was such, and slavery was so extensive, that freedom would have only worsened their condition. Greater protection was found in that relationship than could be expected out of it. (4) As Christians, the slaves were accorded all the privileges of the Christian fellowship, so that their civil status was in no way a spiritual hindrance (see the letter to Philemon).

None of these answers satisfies us fully, because as Bruce comments, "Slavery under the best conditions is slavery none the less, and it could not survive where the gospel had free course."[15] It may well be that Paul thought the silent and steady working of the gospel in the social structure, changing the lives of masses of men and thereby introducing the new principle of liberty, would eventually extirpate slavery.

1. *The duty of slaves* (5-8). Slaves are exhorted to be obedient to their masters. Obedience is the key word. They are not to assume that the new freedom they enjoy in Christ brought to an end their responsibilities in the social system in which they lived. They were, as Summers suggests, "rather to accept the challenge held out before them that being a Christian would make one a better worker in relationship even to human masters."[16]

Their obedience should be characterized in the following ways: *(a) With fear and trembling,* that is, with reverence and proper recognition that their masters can punish them if they do not give a fair day's work; *(b) In singleness of heart,* that is, in sincerity, without hypocrisy, with undivided loyalty as it pertains to the tasks involved; *(c) As unto Christ,* that is, with an obedience regarded as being given first to Christ; *(d) Not with eyeservice, as menpleasers* (6), that is, not performing one's duties busily only when the master is present. Paul wants honesty to be the very essence of their work habits. *(e) With good will doing service, as to the Lord, and not to men* (7-8), that is, they are to serve as Christ's servants, always wanting to fulfill God's will in their daily tasks, difficult though they may be. Their obedience must spring from the heart. Moreover, they should not forget that God is always looking on even though the master may not be present (see 1 Sam. 16:7).

Applying this section to today's workman Barclay comments, "The conviction of the Christian workman is that every single piece of work he produces must be good enough to show to God."[17] It has been suggested that the slave's responsibility may be summed up in these words, "I am a Christian; I must do my best." Furthermore, nothing good done in the name of the Lord is ever lost (8). God will reward His people whatever their status in life and whatever menial, and seemingly degrading work they are called upon to do.

2. *The forbearance of masters* (9). In the Christian com-

munity, where unity and equality must prevail, social responsibilities are to be understood in terms of mutual benefits. Christian masters, therefore, are instructed by the Apostle to *do the same things* as expected of the slaves. This little phrase may refer back to *good will* in verse 7. If so, then the masters are to live by the same Christian principles and to show the same consideration expected of the slaves. Paul adds two specific notes: *(a) Forbearing threatening,* that is, leaving off threats as a means of exacting obedience from slaves, and *(b) Knowing that your Master also is in heaven;* neither *is there respect of persons with him,* which means, "remember you both have the same Master in heaven, and he has no favourites" (NEB).

For people in the Western world, this statement on the relationship of masters and slaves may seem superfluous. But not entirely, for it may speak to employer-employee associations. Surely for the Christian the principles of honest work, of laboring finally for one's Lord, of not using threats to secure maximum production, and of recognizing that all must "give an account of his labor" are applicable. The Christian should so labor as to give no cause for anyone to accuse him of insincerity, unkindness, or laziness.

The Christian Warfare
Ephesians 6:10-20

Warfare seems to be a concept entirely out of keeping with the thought of this Epistle. Paul has been talking about unity and peace, the breaking down of all barriers between men (2:14-22) and the sustaining of society with its diverse human roles through mutual respect and love (5:22—6:9). As Erdman concludes, "If in any of his writings reference to spiritual warfare might be omitted, it would be in the Epistle to the Ephesians."[1]

The Nature of the Foe

Ephesians 6:10-13

> 10 Finally, my brethren, be strong in the Lord, and in the power of his might.
> 11 Put on the whole armour of God, that ye may be able to stand against the wiles of the devil.
> 12 For we wrestle not against flesh and blood, but against principalities, against powers, against the rulers of the darkness of this world, against spiritual wickedness in high places.
> 13 Wherefore take unto you the whole armour of God, that ye may be able to withstand in the evil day, and having done all, to stand.

The clue to the puzzle of Paul's mix of love and warfare is verse 12: "Our fight is not against human foes, but against cosmic powers, against the authorities and potentates of this dark world, against the superhuman forces of evil in the heavens" (NEB). The forces threatening the Christians as they live out their new lives in Christ are not only those which arise out of the human context but also those emanating from the supernatural evil order. Thus, human ingenuity and strength are inadequate to withstand the advance of these powers of evil. God's people need divine might and divine protection to survive. Finally, the battle is the Lord's, and the victory will be His.

1. Paul exhorts the Ephesians to *be strong in the Lord, and in the power of his might* (10). They are to find their strength in the Lord (NEB). He is not suggesting a new surge of power but the drawing upon the strength they already possess through their union with Christ (see 1:19; 3:16). In the conflict with the demonic forces they must draw immediately and continually upon Christ's indwelling power. To *be strong in the Lord* is further explained by the phrase *and in the power of his might.* To be strong in the Lord is to be joined to the strength that belongs to His might. *Power* denotes an active force, whereas *might* denotes a passive force, inherently possessed, whether exercised or not. "Be strong—not in yourself but in the Lord, in the power of his boundless resource" (Phillips). The Christian's preparation for the battle is the Lord himself, who already has dealt a death blow to the forces of evil (Col. 2:15).

2. The enemy of the Christian order is not anything human but the whole evil cosmic structure, actively engaged in defeating Christ's people (11-13). As Vaughn notes, "In military strategy the failure to estimate properly the strength and capabilities of an enemy is a tragic mistake." It is inexcusable for the Christian, for warning has been given as to the nature of the conflict and the formidable character of the enemy. "We are engaged in a life-and-death struggle, not against a frail human enemy but against supernatural forces of evil."[2] *Principalities, powers, rulers of the darkness of this world,* and *spiritual wickedness in high places* (12) are not four different classes of rulers but simply expressions of the one evil power structure.

In high places is literally "in the heavenlies" and suggests the realm of spiritual conflict. No matter how spiritually stable, worshipful, and prayerful God's people might be, they are never immune from attack by the wicked spiritual forces. Paul therefore exhorts his readers to be prepared by wearing "the whole armour of God that you may be able to resist evil in its day of power, and that even when you have fought to a standstill you may still stand your ground" (13, Phillips).

The evil day (13) may be taken to mean "the present age" (see 5:16, "the days are evil") or the particular day when the forces attack. Psalm 41:1 declares, "The Lord will deliver him in time of trouble." Bruce concludes, "The age is evil because of the evil forces which, although vanquished by Christ, are still able to exercise control over a world which will not avail itself of the fruits of Christ's victory."[3]

The Christian's Armor

Ephesians 6:14-20

> 14 Stand therefore, having your loins girt about with truth, and having on the breastplate of righteousness;
> 15 And your feet shod with the preparation of the gospel of peace;
> 16 Above all, taking the shield of faith, wherewith ye shall be able to quench all the fiery darts of the wicked.
> 17 And take the helmet of salvation, and the sword of the Spirit, which is the word of God:
> 18 Praying always with all prayer and supplication in the Spirit, and watching thereunto with all perseverance and supplication for all saints;
> 19 And for me, that utterance may be given unto me, that I may open my mouth boldly, to make known the mystery of the gospel,
> 20 For which I am an ambassador in bonds: that therein I may speak boldly, as I ought to speak.

The Christian must wrap himself in the armor provided by God and, having fastened it securely about him, go out to resist evil in his time.

1. *The armor God provides is more than adequate for the battle* (14-17). *Whole armour* translates the Greek word *panoplia* which can either mean "splendid armor" or "complete armor." The former translations is suggested by Barth because he concludes that the word *panoplia* sug-

gests a public display of the qualities of truth, righteousness, peace, and faith.[4] However, the element of completeness seems more appropriate since Paul is concerned in this passage to call Christians to dependence upon God's power for victory over wickedness. While, as John Bunyan has noted in his *Pilgrim's Progress,* the armor offers no protection to the back, the expectation of Paul is that the Christian has no defense anyhow if he retreats from trusting the Lord.

The various pieces of the armor are Christian graces. *Truth* is the girdle and *righteousness* is the breastplate. *Truth* is to be understood here not as the gospel in the objective sense but the gospel as being lived by faith. The Christian soldier lives in truth, faithfulness, loyalty, and sincerity. *Righteousness* refers to right conduct or practice, rather than the righteous status the believer knows through faith in Christ. In Isa. 59:17, the prophet pictures God as putting on "righteousness as a breastplate, and a helmet of salvation upon his head." *The breastplate of righteousness* suggests the protecting quality of holiness. Barclay writes, "When a man is clothed in righteousness, he is impregnable. Words are no defence against accusation, but a good life is."[5]

The Christian warrior must have the protection and mobility which come with having the *feet shod with the preparation of the gospel of peace* (15). Isaiah's majestic words break through here: "How beautiful upon the mountains are the feet of him who brings good tidings, who publishes peace, who brings good tidings of good, who publishes salvation; who says to Zion, 'Your God reigns!'" (52:7, RSV). The Christian is a bearer of God's good news of peace—peace between God and man and between man and his fellowmen (cf. 2:17). This is his only adequate preparation for the battle.

Roman soldiers carried a large, oblong shield carved of wood and covered with leather so as to intercept and quench the ignited arrows of the enemy. The Christian warrior carries a shield of faith, which symbolizes a trusting relationship with God. "Every burning missile the enemy hurls" (Phillips) can be stopped by a continuing commitment in faith to God.

The helmet of salvation (17a) does not refer to the great confidence that God has power to save, but rather to the protection which participation in God's salvation assures. If a soldier goes into the battle estranged from God, without knowledge and confidence in his Leader, he has no guarantee of protection in the heat of the battle. On the other hand, the grace of God will make him "more than conqueror." "If God be for us, who can be against us?" (Rom. 8:31; see also 8:37-39). First Thessalonians 5:8 speaks of the helmet as "the hope of salvation." Westcott states the point tersely: "The sense of salvation puts life beyond all danger."[6]

In his hand the Christian warrior wields *the sword of the Spirit, which is the word of God* (17b). The sword is the property of the Spirit and is the written Word of God, the Holy Scriptures. It is the Spirit who inspired the Word (2 Tim. 3:16; 2 Pet. 1:20-21) and who now interprets the Word to believers. Our Lord effectively wielded the Word in overcoming Satan's temptations in the wilderness. All the other pieces of the armor are for defense, but *the sword of the Spirit* is the one offensive weapon. Wesley comments: "We are to attack Satan, as well as secure ourselves; the shield in one hand, and the sword in the other. Whoever fights with the powers of hell will need both."[7] We must remember that "the word of God is quick, and powerful, and sharper than any twoedged sword" (Heb. 4:12).

2. *Persistent prayer must characterize the life of the Christian warrior as he engages the enemy* (18-20). Prayer must be ceaseless *(always)*, earnest *(with all perseverance)*, and selfless *(for all saints)*. All the saints are in the battle against evil and each one needs to be "held up in prayer" in order that he may remain strong in the battle. The main responsibility of the Christian in this fight is to

have boldness in declaring the Word of the Lord (19-20). Paul especially needs their prayers, since he is bound in chains in Rome. However, he sees his condition as one in which he is *an ambassador in bonds* (20). Even though the enemy may conclude that one of his major opponents has been successfully restrained, the Apostle is confident that the Word of the Lord will eventually prevail. But he needs the support of his fellow soldiers in prayer that he will not fail to give open testimony to his faith.

Too much cannot be said about the necessity of prayer in the life of the Christian and the church. Prayer brings God near, releases the resources of God for the battle, and enables the Christian to stand even when he thinks he cannot stay on his feet any longer.

Paul's Farewell
Ephesians 6:21-24

Ephesians 6:21-24

> 21 But that ye also may know my affairs, and how I do, Tychicus, a beloved brother and faithful minister in the Lord, shall make known to you all things:
> 22 Whom I have sent unto you for the same purpose, that ye might know our affairs, and that he might comfort your hearts.
> 23 Peace be to the brethren, and love with faith, from God the Father and the Lord Jesus Christ.
> 24 Grace be with all them that love our Lord Jesus Christ in sincerity. Amen.
> Written from Rome unto the Ephesians by Tychicus

We have said this letter is probably a circular letter and one of the reasons for that conclusion is the absence of greetings to a number of friends so typical of Paul's other letters. In this letter Paul stimply states that *Tychicus, a beloved brother* and *faithful minister* (21) will deliver the letter and will tell them about his affairs, how things are going with him, perhaps a reference to his legal battles and his health. The pastoral sensitivity of the Apostle breaks through here as he sends this information about himself, not for any personal benefit but that the hearts of his friends might be comforted. He was so close to them in spirit he seems to intuit that they might be spiritually disturbed over his situation in prison (22).

The letter closes with a benediction much like the greeting at the beginning. *Peace, love with faith* and *grace* (23-24) are the three great qualities of the Christian life which Paul elucidates throughout this Epistle. *Peace* is the blessing of reconciliation which union with Christ bestows. *Love* is the beneficent quality of one's life when Christ dwells within. *Grace* is the unmerited favor of God which made possible the new life and subsequently sustains it. Paul prays that God's favor will be continually expressed to them, in them, and through them as they continue to love the Lord Jesus Christ with an unfailing love.

Reference Notes

The Epistle to the Galatians

THE AUTHENTICITY OF PAUL'S GOSPEL

1. Herman N. Ridderbos, "The Epistle of Paul to the Churches of Galatia," *The New International Commentary of the New Testament,* (Grand Rapids: Wm. B. Eerdmans Publishing Co., 1953), p. 46.

2. Joachim Jeremias, *The Central Message of the New Testament* (New York: Charles Scribner's Sons, 1965), p. 46.

3. J. B. Lightfoot, *The Epistle of St. Paul to the Galatians* (Grand Rapids: Zondervan Publishing House, 1975, Reprint), p. 76.

4. William Neil, "The Letter of Paul to the Galatians," *The Cambridge Bible Commentary,* (Cambridge: University Press, 1967), p. 24.

5. Ernest DeWitt Burton, "The Epistle to the Galatians," *The International Critical Commentary* (Edinburgh: T. & T. Clark, 1921), p. 40.

6. Ibid., p. 46.

7. R. A. Cole, "Galatians," *Tyndale New Testament Commentaries* (Grand Rapids: Wm. B. Eerdmans Publishing Co., 1965), p. 51.

8. Ibid., pp. 51-52.

9. Ibid., p. 60.

10. Andrew W. Blackwood, Jr., *Galatians,* (Grand Rapids: Baker Book House, 1962), p. 28. '

11. Hans Dieter Betz, "Galatians," *Hermeneia,* (Philadelphia: Fortress Press, 1979), p. 95.

12. Cole, "Galatians" (TNTC), p. 69.

13. Ralph P. Martin, "1 and 2 Corinthians-Galatians," *Bible Study Books* (Grand Rapids: Wm. B. Eerdmans Publishing Co., 1968), p. 105.

14. Martin, "1 and 2 Corinthians-Galatians" (BSB), p. 105.

15. Betz, "Galatians," p. 107.

16. Neil, "Galatians" (CBC), p. 41.

17. Betz, "Galatians," p. 110.

18. Blackwood, *Galatians,* p. 31.

19. Betz, "Galatians," p. 112

20. Ibid.

21. Cole, "Galatians" (TNTC), p. 79.

22. Ibid. p. 80.

23. R. E. Howard, "Galatians," *Beacon Bible Commentary* (Kansas City: Beacon Hill Press of Kansas City, 1965), 9:51.

24. Ibid, p. 82.

THE PROOF OF HISTORY

1. Neil, "Galatians" (CBC), p. 47.

2. Martin, "1 and 2 Corinthians—Galatians," p. 109.

3. Ibid., p. 110.

4. Blackwood, *Galatians,* p. 41.

5. Martin, "1 and 2 Corinthians-Galatians" (BSB), p. 111.

6. Neil, "Galatians" (CBC), pp. 56-57.

7. Cole "Galatians" (TNTC), p. 103.

8. Martin, "1 and 2 Corinthians-Galatians" (BSB), p. 112.

9. Ibid., p. 113.

10. Ibid.

11. Neil, "Galatians" (CBC), p. 61.

12. Betz, "Galatians," p. 186.

13. William Barclay, "The Letters to the Galatians and Ephesians." *The Daily Study Bible Series,* Second edition (Philadelphia: Westminster Press, 1958), p. 25.

14. Cole, "Galatians" (TNTC), pp. 113-14; see Heb. 5:12; Col. 2:8, 20.

15. Neil, "Galatians" (CBC), p. 64.

16. Ibid., p. 65.

17. Ibid., pp. 65-66.

18. Adam Clarke, "Galatians," *The New Testament of Our Lord and Saviour Jesus Christ with a Commentary* (Nashville; Abingdon Press, n.d., reprint), 6:403.

19. Neil, "Galatians" (CBC), p. 67.

20. Howard, "Galatians" (BBC), 9:71.

21. Ibid.

22. Ridderbos, "Churches of Galatia" (NICNT), p. 161.

23. Barclay, "Galatians and Ephesians" (DSB), p. 40.

24. Blackwood, *Galatians,* p. 58.

25. Martin, "1 and 2 Corinthians-Galatians" (BSB), p. 117.

26. Frank Stagg, "Galatians-Romans," *Knox Preaching Guides* (Atlanta: John Knox Press, 1980), p. 23.

27. Cole "Galatians" (TNTC), p. 127.

28. Stagg, "Galatians-Romans" (KPG), p. 25.

29. Cole, "Galatians" (TNTC), p. 136.

THE LIFE OF FREEDOM

1. Stagg, "Galatians-Romans" (KPG), p. 26.

2. Betz, "Galatians," p. 256.

3. Neil, "Galatians" (CBC), pp. 73-74.

4. Martin, "1 and 2 Corinthians-Galatians" (BSB), p. 119.

5. Clarke, "Galatians," 6:409.

6. Betz, "Galatians," p. 261.

7. Martin Luther, *A Commentary on St. Paul's Epistle to the Galatians,* abridged tr. by Theodore Graebner (2nd. ed.; Grand Rapids: Zondervan Publishing House, n.d.), p. 204.

8. Howard, "Galatians" (BBC), 9:86-87.

9. George S. Duncan, "The Epistle of Paul to the Galatians," *The Moffatt New Testament Commentary* (New York: Harper and Bros., 1934), p. 163.

10. Martin, "1 and 2 Corinthians-Galatians" (BSB), p. 121.

11. Howard, "Galatians" (BBC), 9:91.

12. Ibid., 9:94.

13. John Wesley, *Explanatory Notes upon the New Testament* (Naperville, Ill.: Alec Allenson, 1950, reprint), p. 697.

14. Betz, "Galatians," p. 22.

15. William Barclay, *Flesh and Spirit* (London: SCM Press, 1962), p. 21.

16. Clarke, "Galatians," 6:413.

17. Ibid.

18. J. Oswald Sanders, *The Holy Spirit and His Gifts,* rev. ed. (Grand Rapids: Zondervan Publishing House, 1970), p. 152.

19. Ridderbos, "Galatians" (NICNT), p. 208.

20. Howard, "Galatians" (BBC), 9:110-11.

21. A. W. Tozer, *The Pursuit of God* (Harrisburg, Pa.: Christian Publications, 1948), pp. 22, 44-45.

FREEDOM TO SERVE OTHERS

1. Neil "Galatians" (CBC), p. 83.

2. J. H. Jowett, *My Daily Meditation* (La Verne, CA.: El Camino Press, 1975, reprint), p. 163.

3. Ibid.

4. Blackwood, *Galatians,* p. 82.

5. Jowett, *Daily Meditation,* p. 163.

6. Blackwood, *Galatians,* p. 83.

7. L. Harold DeWolf, *Galatians, a Letter for Today* (Grand Rapids: Wm. B. Eerdmans Publishing Co., 1971), p. 79.

8. Frank Stagg, "Freedom and Moral Responsibility without License or Legalism," *Review and Expositor,* LXIX (Fall, 1972), p. 492.

9. Howard, "Galatians" (BBC), 9:116.

10. DeWolf, *Galatians,* p. 81.

11. Neil, "Galatians" (CBC), p. 85.

12. Ibid., p. 86.

POSTSCRIPT

1. Cole, "Galatians" (TNTC), pp. 181-82.
2. Neil, "Galatians" (CBC), p. 88.

The Epistle to the Ephesians

Introduction

1. F. F. Bruce, *The Epistle to the Ephesians* (New York: Fleming H. Revell Co., 1961), pp. 11-12.

2. John Mackay, *God's Order: The Ephesian Letter and This Present Time* (New York: The Macmillan Co., 1953), pp 6-7.

A Christian Greeting

1. G. G. Findlay, "Ephesians-Philippians," *Expositor's Bible* (EB) (New York: A. C. Armstrong and Son, 1903), p. 3.

2. R. W. Dale, *Lectures on Ephesians* (London: Hodder and Stoughton, 1887), p. 13.

3. Ray Summers, *Ephesians: Pattern for Christian Living* (Nashville: Broadman Press, 1960), p. 8.

A Hymn of Salvation

1. Findlay, "Ephesians-Philippians" (EB), p. 21.

2. Curtis Vaughn, "Ephesians," *A Study Guide Commentary* (Grand Rapids: Zondervan Publishing House, 1977), p. 18.

3. Ibid., p. 19.

4. J. Armitage Robinson, *St. Paul's Epistle to the Ephesians* (rev. ed.; London: Macmillan & Co., 1903), p. 26.

5. Francis Foulkes, "The Epistle of Paul to the Ephesians," *The Tyndale New Testament Commentaries* (TNTC), (Grand Rapids: Wm. B. Eerdmans Publishing Co., 1963), p. 47.

6. Adam Clarke, "Ephesians," *The New Testament of Our Lord and Saviour Jesus Christ* (New York: Abingdon Cokesbury Press, n.d.), 6:431.

7. Markus Barth, "Ephesians 1—3, Ephesians 4—6," *The Anchor Bible* (Garden City, N.Y.: Doubleday & Co., 1974), p. 109.

8. Mackay, *God's Order*, p. 68.

9. Norman H. Snaith, "Choose, Chosen, Elect, Election," *Theological Workbook of the Bible*, ed. Alan Richardson (London: SCM Press, 1950), p. 44.

10. Dale, *Lectures on Ephesians*, pp. 31-32.

11. Bruce, *Ephesians*, pp. 29-30.

12. Dale, *Lectures on Ephesians,* p. 63.

13. Foulkes, "Ephesians" (TNTC), p. 50.

14. Bruce, *Ephesians,* p. 32.

15. Foulkes, "Ephesians" (TNTC), p. 21.

16. Vaughn, "Ephesians," p. 26.

17. John Wesley, *Explanatory Notes upon the New Testament* (London: Epworth Press, 1950 reprint).

18. Ralph Earle, *Word Meanings in the New Testament* (Kansas City: Beacon Hill Press of Kansas City, 1979), 4:242.

A Prayer for Enlightenment

1. Bruce, *Ephesians,* p. 38.

2. Summers, *Ephesians,* p. 27.

3. Ibid., p. 28.

4. B. F. Westcott, *St. Paul's Epistle to the Ephesians* (Grand Rapids: Wm. B. Eerdmans Publishing Co., 1950 reprint), p. 24.

5. Bruce, *Ephesians,* p. 41.

6. Mackay, *God's Order,* p. 94.

The Creation of a New People

1. Findlay, "Ephesians-Philippians" (EB), p. 96.

2. Earle, *Word Meanings,* 4:266.

3. Barth, "Ephesians 1-3" (AB), p. 213.

4. Foulkes, "Ephesians" (TNTC), p. 70; see Col. 3:6.

5. S. D. F. Salmond, "Ephesians," *The Expositor's Greek Testament* (EGT), (London: Hodder and Stoughton, n.d.), 3:285.

6. Vaughn, *Ephesians,* p. 47.

7. William Hendriksen, "Ephesians," *New Testament Commentary* (Grand Rapids: Baker Book House, 1967), p. 115.

8. Findlay, "Ephesians-Philippians" (EB), p. 105.

9. Barth, "Ephesians 1-3" (AB), p. 219.

10. Findlay, "Ephesians-Philippians" (EB), p. 106.

11. Ibid., p. 113.

12. Vaughn, "Ephesians," p. 53; see Titus 2:14; 3:8.

13. Mackay, *God's Order,* p. 25; see William Barclay, "The

Letters to the Galatians and Ephesians," *The Daily Study Bible,* 2nd ed. (Philadelphia: Westminster Press, 1958), p. 125.

14. Markus Barth, *The Broken Wall: A Study of the Epistle to the Ephesians* (London: Collins, 1960), p. 36.

15. Ibid., p. 37.

16. Foulkes, "Ephesians" (TNTC), p. 83.

17. Francis W. Beare, "Ephesians," *Interpreter's Bible* (IB), ed. George Buttrick, et al., (New York: Abingdon-Cokesbury Press, 1953), 10:659.

18. Ibid., 10:600.

19. Wesley, *Notes,* p. 709.

20. Mackay, *God's Order,* p. 131.

21. Findlay, "Ephesians-Philippians" (EB), p. 153.

A Prayer for Divine Fullness

1. John R. W. Stott, *God's New Society: The Message of Ephesians* (Downers Grove, Ill.: InterVarsity Press, 1979), p. 114.

2. A. Leonard Griffith, *Ephesians, A Positive Affirmation* (Waco, Tex.: Word Books, 1975), p. 55.

3. Barth, "Ephesians 1—3" (AB), p. 361.

4. Stott, *God's New Society,* p. 117.

5. Ibid., p. 118.

6. Beare, "Ephesians" (IB), 10:669.

7. Westcott, *Ephesians,* p. 48.

8. Stott, *God's New Society,* p. 126.

9. Handley C. G. Moule, *Veni Creator* (London: Hodder and Stoughton, 1890), p. 228.

10. D. Martyn Lloyd-Jones, *The Unsearchable Riches of Christ* (Grand Rapids: Baker Book House, 1979), pp. 117-18.

11. Ibid., p. 131.

12. H. C. G. Moule, *Ephesian Studies* (2nd ed., London: Pickering and Inglis, Ltd., n.d.), p. 129.

13. Dale, *Lectures on Ephesians,* p. 250.

14. Summers, *Ephesians,* p. 66.

15. Stott, *God's New Society,* p. 137.

16. Charles Hodge, *Commentary on the Epistle to the*

Ephesians (Grand Rapids: Wm. B. Eerdmans Publishing Co., 1950), p. 190.

17. Adam Clarke, *Theology* (New York: J. Collard, 1837), p. 192.

18. Alfred Martin, "Ephesians," *Wycliffe Bible Commentary* (Chicago: Moody Press, 1962), p. 1023.

The Unity of the Church

1. Barth, *The Broken Wall,* p. 200.
2. Hodge, *Ephesians,* p. 200.
3. Mackay, *God's Order,* p. 136.
4. Summers, *Ephesians,* p. 79.
5. Dale, *Lectures on Ephesians,* p. 323.
6. Stott, *God's New Society,* p. 159.
7. Ibid.
8. Salmond, "Ephesians" (EGT), 3:333.
9. Summers, *Ephesians,* p. 89.

The Old Life and the New

1. Dale, *Lectures in Ephesians,* p. 296.
2. Ibid., p. 90.
3. Vaughn, "Ephesians," p. 100.
4. E. F. Scott, "The Epistles of Paul to the Colossians, to Philemon, and to the Ephesians," *Moffatt New Testament Commentaries* (New York: Harper and Bros., 1930), p. 218.
5. A. M. Hunter, "The Letter of Paul to the Ephesians," *Laymen's Bible Commentary* (LBC), (Richmond, Va.: John Knox Press, 1959), p. 68.
6. Bruce, *Ephesians,* p. 95.
7. Stott, *God's New Society,* p. 184.
8. These headings are taken from Stott, ibid., pp. 184-90.
9. Summers, *Ephesians,* p. 89.

Living as the Beloved

1. This descriptive phrase was suggested by Barth, *The Broken Wall,* p. 159.
2. Barth, "Ephesians 4—6" (AB), pp. 556-57.

3. Mackay, *God's Order,* p. 170.

4. Salmond, "Ephesians" (EGT), 3:350.

5. Barth, "Ephesians 4—6" (AB), p. 559.

6. Scott, "Ephesians" (MNTC), p. 227.

7. Beare, "Ephesians" (IB), 10:709.

8. Scott, "Ephesians" (MNTC), p. 230.

9. Beare, "Ephesians" (IB), 10:711.

10. Barclay, "Galatians-Ephesians" (DSB), p. 196.

11. Vaughn, "Ephesians," p. 110.

12. Stott, *God's New Society,* p. 208.

CHRISTIAN RELATIONSHIPS

1. Westcott, *Ephesians,* pp. 82-83.

2. Stott, *God's New Society,* p. 217.

3. Barth, "Ephesians 4—6" (AB), p. 756.

4. Beare, "Ephesians" (IB), 10:720.

5. Foulkes, "Ephesians" (TNTC), p. 157.

6. Bruce, *Ephesians,* p. 115.

7. Beare, "Ephesians" (IB), 10:724.

8. Summers, *Ephesians,* p. 127.

9. Salmond, "Ephesians" (EGT), 3:375.

10. Wedel, "Ephesians," (Exposition) (IB), 10:731.

11. Stott, *God's New Society,* p. 241.

12. Hodge, *Ephesians,* p. 359.

13. Findlay, "Ephesians-Philippians" (EB), p. 386.

14. Beare, "Ephesians" (IB), 10:732.

15. Bruce, *Ephesians,* 125.

16. Summers, *Ephesians,* p. 133.

17. Barclay, "Galatians-Ephesians" (DSB), p. 215.

THE CHRISTIAN WARFARE

1. Charles R. Erdman, *The Epistle of Paul to the Ephesians* (Philadelphia: Westminster Press, 1931), p. 121.

2. Vaughn, "Ephesians," p. 126.

3. Bruce, *Ephesians,* p. 129.

4. Barth, "Ephesians 4-6" (AB), p. 793.

5. Barclay, "Galatians-Ephesians" (DSB), p. 217.
6. Westcott, *Ephesians,* p. 97.
7. Wesley, *Notes,* p. 723.

Bibliographies

GALATIANS

Barclay, William. "The Letters to the Galatians and Ephesians," *The Daily Study Bible Series*. 2nd Edition. Philadelphia: Westminster Press, 1958.

———. *Flesh and Spirit*. London: SCM Press, 1962.

Betz, Hans Dieter. "Galatians," *Hermeneia*. Philadelphia: Fortress Press, 1979.

Blackwood, Andrew W., Jr. *Galatians*. Grand Rapids: Baker Book House, 1962.

Burton, Ernest DeWitt. "The Epistle to the Galatians." *The International Critical Commentary*. Edinburgh: T. & T. Clark, 1921.

Clarke, Adam. "Galatians," *The New Testament of Our Lord and Saviour Jesus Christ*. New York: Abingdon-Cokesbury Press, n.d. (reprint).

Cole, R. A. "The Epistle of Paul to the Galatians," *Tyndale New Testament Commentaries*. Grand Rapids: Wm. B. Eerdmans Publishing Co., 1965.

DeWolf, L. Harold. *Galatians, a Letter for Today*. Grand Rapids: Wm. B. Eerdmans Publishing Co., 1971.

Duncan, George S. "The Epistle of Paul to the Galatians," *The Moffatt New Testament Commentary*. New York: Harper and Bros., 1934.

Howard, Richard E. "The Epistle to the Galatians," *Beacon Bible Commentary*. Vol. IX. Kansas City, Mo.: Beacon Hill Press of Kansas City, 1965.

Jeremias, Joachim. *The Central Message of the New Testament*. New York: Charles Scribner's Sons, 1965.

Jowett, J. H. *My Daily Meditation*. LaVerne, Ca.: El Camino Press, 1975, (reprint).

Lightfoot, J. B. *The Epistle of St. Paul to the Galatians.* Grand
Rapids: Zondervan Publishing House, 1957 (reprint).

Luther, Martin. *A Commentary on St. Paul's Epistle to the
Galatians.* Abridged, trans. Theodore Graebner. 2nd Edition, Grand Rapids: Zondervan Publishing House, n.d.

Martin, Ralph P. "1 and 2 Corinthians, Galatians", *Bible
Study Books.* Grand Rapids: Wm. B. Eerdmans Publishing
Co., 1968.

Neil, William. "The Letter of Paul to the Galatians," *Cambridge Bible Commentary.* Cambridge: University Press,
1967.

Ridderbos, Herman N. "The Epistle of Paul to the Churches of
Galatia," *The New International Commentary on the New
Testament.* Grand Rapids: Wm. B. Eerdmans Publishing
Co., 1953.

Sanders, J. Oswald. *The Holy Spirit and His Gifts.* Rev. ed.
Grand Rapids: Zondervan Publishing House, 1970.

Stagg, Frank. "Galatians-Romans," *Knox Preaching Guides.*
Atlanta: John Knox Press, 1980.

_____. "Freedom and Moral Responsibility Without License or
Legalism," *Review and Expositor.* LXIX (Fall, 1972).

Wesley, John. *Explanatory Notes upon the New Testament.*
Naperville, Ill.: Alec Allenson, 1950. (Reprint).

EPHESIANS

Barclay, William "The Letters to the Galatians and Ephesians."
2nd ed. *The Daily Study Bible.* Philadelphia: Westminster
Press, 1958.

Barth, Markus. *The Broken Wall: A Study of the Epistle to the
Ephesians.* London: Collins, 1960.

_____. "Ephesians 1—3, Ephesians 4—6," *The Anchor Bible*
(AB). Garden City, N.Y.: Doubleday and Co., 1974.

Beare, Francis W. "Ephesians" (Exegesis). *Interpreter's Bible*
(IB). Edited by George Buttrick, *et al.,* Vol. X. New York:
Abingdon-Cokesbury Press, 1953.

Bruce, F. F. *The Epistle to the Ephesians.* New York: Fleming
H. Revell Co., 1961.

Carver, W. O. *The Glory of God in the Christian Calling.* Nashville: Broadman Press, 1949.

Clarke, Adam. "Ephesians," *The New Testament of our Lord and Saviour Jesus Christ,* Vol. VI. New York: Abingdon-Cokesbury Press, n.d.

———. *Theology.* New York: J. Collard, 1837.

Dale, R. W. *Lectures on Ephesians.* London: Hodder and Stoughton, 1887.

Earle, Ralph. *Word Meanings in the New Testament.* Kansas City: Beacon Hill Press of Kansas City, 1979.

Findlay, G. G. "Ephesians—Philippians," *Expositor's Bible* (EB). New York: A. C. Armstrong and Son, 1903.

Foulkes, Francis. "The Epistle of Paul to the Ephesians," *The Tyndale New Testament Commentaries* (TC). Grand Rapids: Wm. B. Eerdmans Publishing House, 1963.

Griffith, A. Leonard. *Ephesians: A Positive Affirmation.* Waco, Texas: Word Books, 1975.

Hendriksen, William. "Ephesians," *New Testament Commentary* (NTC). Grand Rapids: Baker Book House, 1967.

Hodge, Charles. *Commentary on the Epistle to the Ephesians.* Grand Rapids: Wm. B. Eerdmans Publishing Co., 1950.

Hunter, A. M. "The Letter of Paul to the Ephesians." *Layman's Bible Commentary* (LBC). Richmond, Va.: John Knox Press, 1959.

Lloyd-Jones, D. Martyn. *The Unsearchable Riches of Christ.* Grand Rapids: Baker Book House, 1979.

Mackay, John. *God's Order: The Ephesian Letter and This Present Time.* New York: The Macmillan Co., 1953.

Martin, Alfred. "Ephesians," *Wycliffe Bible Commentary.* Chicago: Moody Press, 1962.

Moule, H. C. G. *Veni Creator.* London: Hodder and Stoughton, 1890.

———. *Ephesian Studies.* 2nd ed., London: Pickering and Inglis, Ltd., n.d.

Richardson, Alan (ed.) *Theological Wordbook of the Bible.* London: SCM Press, 1950.

Robinson, J. Armitage. *St. Paul's Epistle to the Ephesians.* Rev. ed., London: Macmillan & Co., 1903.

Salmond, S. D. F. "Ephesians," *The Expositor's Greek Testament* (EGT), Vol. III. London: Hodder and Stoughton, n.d.

Scott, E. F. "The Epistles of Paul to the Colossians, to Philemon, and to the Ephesians," *Moffatt New Testament Commentary*. New York: Harper and Bros., 1930.

Stott, John R. W. *God's New Society: The Message of Ephesians*. Downers Grove, Ill.: InterVarsity Press, 1979.

Summers, Ray. *Ephesians: Pattern for Christian Living*. Nashville: Broadman Press, 1960.

Vaughn, Curtis. "Ephesians," *A Study Guide Commentary*. Grand Rapids: Zondervan Publishing House, 1977.

Wedel, Theodore, "Ephesians" (Exposition), *Interpreter's Bible* Edited by George Buttrick, *et al.,* Vol. X, New York: Abingdon-Cokesbury Press, 1953.

Wesley, John. *Explanatory Notes Upon the New Testament*. London: Epworth Press, 1950 (reprint).

Westcott, B. F. *St. Paul's Epistle to the Ephesians*. Grand Rapids: Wm. B. Eerdmans Publishing Co., 1950 (reprint).